About the Author

Adrienne Brady was born in Burma and grew up in Surrey. Marriage and four children took care of her creative energies for a good number of years. An Honours Degree in English and History and a Master's Degree in Creative Writing acted as a springboard for writing her own poetry and to satisfy a deep rooted ambition for travel and travel writing. Since 1987 she has lived overseas in Singapore, Brunei, Libya and the Middle East taking opportunities to explore ancient and lost worlds as well as to capture them in words and on camera.

Based in Dubai from 1996-2006 her travel features were published regularly in Gulf newspapers and magazines. From a home base in Devon and more recently Dorset, she has continued to travel as well as completing two memoirs of life and travels in Libya under sanctions and travels throughout Oman and into Central Africa. *Danger Zones and Pleasure Zones* takes a leap back in time to explorations in Asia, then forward to the Gulf and Europe to complete a fascinating trilogy of adventures through a complex and dramatically changing world.

For Mark, Catriona, Fiona & Justine

Adrienne Brady

DANGER ZONES
&
PLEASURE ZONES

- *Shifting Horizons* -

AUSTIN MACAULEY
PUBLISHERS LTD

A CIP catalogue record for this title is available from the British Library.

ISBN 978 1 78455 368 5 (Paperback)
ISBN 978 1 78455 370 8 (Hardback)
ISBN 978 1 78455 369 2 (E-Book)

www.austinmacauley.com

First Published (2016)
Austin Macauley Publishers Ltd.
25 Canada Square
Canary Wharf
London
E14 5LB

Acknowledgments

As always it is the people I travelled with and stayed with who made my expeditions not only possible but are the reason why I am still here and still travelling. I am indebted to Patrick, expatriate friend in Colombo, who provided me with a safe and lovely place to stay between my travels throughout Sri Lanka; the Dutch couple who invited me to travel with them through Tamil controlled territory to visit the magnificent Buddhist sites of Sri Lanka's Golden Triangle; fellow sailors – captain and crew of the 38' sailing yacht, *The Star of Siam* – with whom I shared the hazards as well as the thrills on a two week trip round the Philippine Island of Palawan. Further thanks to fellow expatriates in Libya – without their company I would have been confined to life behind the walls of a residential compound. Karen, friend and work colleague in Abu Dhabi, for her company trekking in Nepal.

This is also in memory of my late partner and travel companion, Richard (Chapman) who lost his life to cancer in 2008; Richard was an invaluable part of my life and travels from bases in the Emirates and the UK. I miss him with all my heart. Finally, my gratitude and love to my daughters Catriona, Fiona and Justine for sharing life-changing travel experiences to some of the most beautiful as well as some of the wildest places off the beaten trail.

Once again I am indebted to the following: Andy McTiernan and Julie Bell – management and editing team of *Property World Middle East* and the editing teams of *Khaleej Times* and *Friday Magazine,*

(Gulf News), Dubai – for the splendid presentations of those travel features and photographs that form the basis of the memoir; Catriona and Justine for memories and editing suggestions of accounts of our unexpected adventures in Sabah; my granddaughter Jasmine Elizabeth for her creative work on the cover design and map; friend and Editorial Consultant, Rodger Witt for unfailing insightful comments and suggestions.

In some instances the names of people I travelled with or encountered have been changed to protect identities. I have drawn upon a wide variety of sources during my travels and since. Opinions and errors are mine. I am especially indebted to the writings of those authors mentioned in the Selective Bibliography. As a result of the time span and long-distance overseas postings and travels – apart from the invaluable *Insight Guides* – I have been unable to trace a number of the sources referred to on my earlier travels. Every effort has been made in this field as well as to contact the copyright holders of quoted material. Late responses and inadvertent omissions will be rectified in future editions.

Last but not least, my gratitude to Annette Longman and Robert Brookes and the editorial, production and promotion team of Austin Macauley for bringing *Danger Zones and Pleasure Zones* to fruition; especial thanks to Neil Burrows and Vinh Tran for their patience and advice.

Annotated outline map of Asia, thanks to Jasmine E. Brady

Extract from *Foucault's Pendulum* by Umberto Eco reprinted by permission of Tom Atkins, Random House

Singapore Plus: First published as *Any Mo Kui* in 'Quintet' by Staple First Editions, 1993)

Desert Rose & Do-it-yourself Tourism: First published in 'Kiss The Hand You Cannot Sever' (Melrose Books, Cambridgeshire, UK, 2008)

The Magic of Musandam first published in 'Way South of Wahiba Sands' (Austin Macauley Publishers, Canary Wharf, London, 2013)

Contents

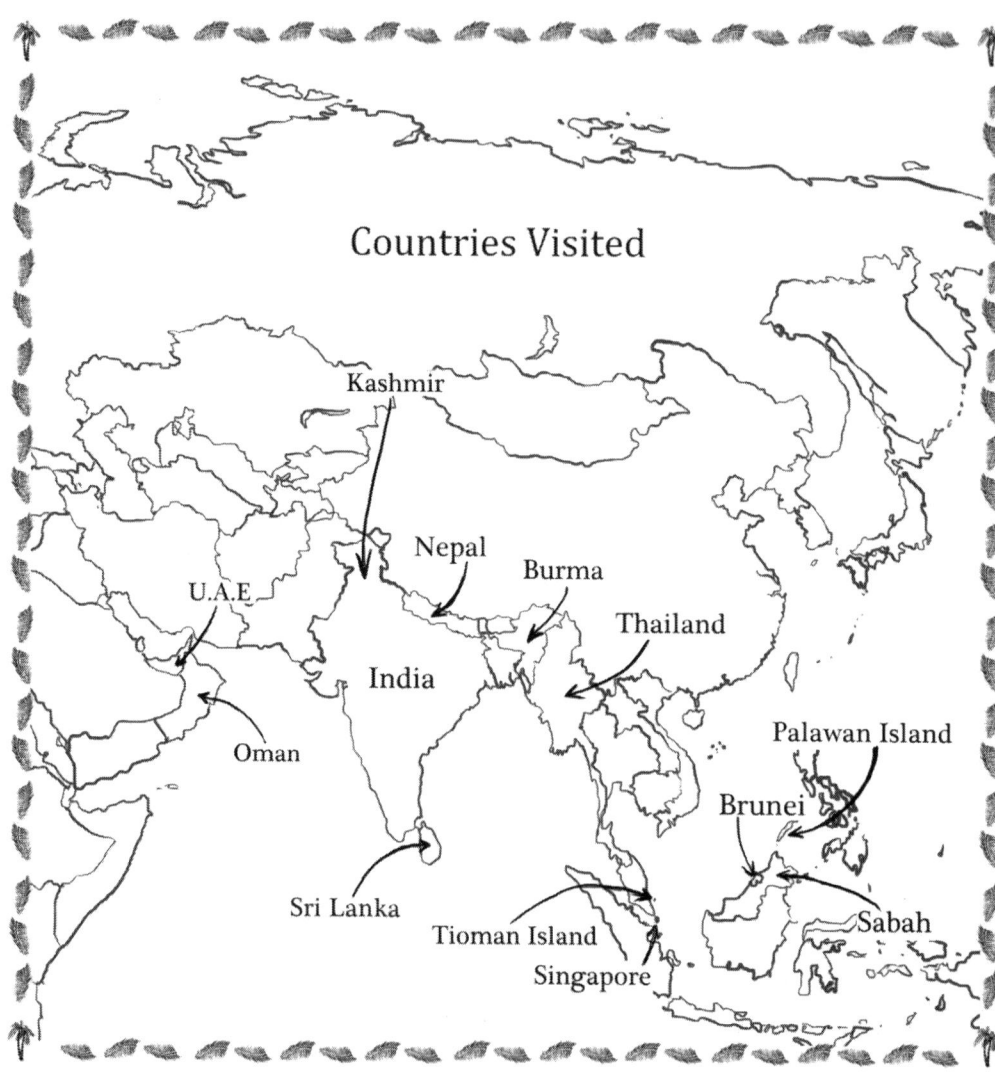
Countries Visited

Foreword

It was on my return from a final overseas posting to live in the UK in 2006 that I set about converting those travel features – previously published in Gulf newspapers and magazines – into a trilogy of memoirs of my travels: Asia, then Libya followed by the UAE, Oman and Africa. Then unforeseen circumstances intervened. It was while I was working on *Danger Zones & Pleasure Zones* that Libya was making world news. Gaddafi had agreed to hand over the Lockerbie suspects and to end the weapons of mass destruction programme, releasing the country from imposed sanctions: Libya's doors were opened to the outside world. Knowing that I had unique firsthand experience of life in Libya under sanctions I put *Danger Zones* to one side, to focus on and complete *Kiss The Hand You Cannot Sever*.

Once again as I set about working on travels in Asia things did not go according to plan: cancer took the life of my partner and travel companion, Richard Chapman. *Way South of Wahiba Sands* – an account of my travels with Richard, took priority and Asia was put on hold for the second time.

At last the trilogy is complete taking the reader full circle. From a base in Singapore, the highs and lows of my adventures are centered on explorations in Sri Lanka, Kashmir, Borneo and Thailand. Life and travels from jungle clad Brunei contrast with a visit to Libya's desert based city of Ghadames. Then the safety and convenience of a base in the United Arab Emirates opened doors to excursions to Nepal, Malaysia and Oman. Finally, visits to Andalusia and Galway from my Dorset home bring the memoir to a close.

An interweaving of travel poems, between chapters, captures not just the surface features but the innermost nature of the countries visited as well as the emotions they stir. *Singapore Plus* opens the memoir preparing the reader for travels through Asia's rapidly changing world.

Singapore Plus

I live on an island, fifteen hours
as the swallow flies from home,
on the fifteenth floor of a high-rise
high technological block.
They've scooped the hills
into the sea. It's perfectly flat
for perfectly straight sky-scrapers
to grow side by side. Every day
I dream about horizons.

Don't say we didn't warn you.
It's time to settle. Think
about the children.

My children come out of the sky.
We spend our days on the sea
learning the rootless language of waves.

There are no seasons. Daylight
clocks on: clocks off. All year,

day and night, fans churn sluggish heat.
I've never believed in saunas.
My body grows as soft as the cells
of my brain. I've lost all perimeters.

I sleep to the sound of sucked in rushing
wind. Guard dogs are howling.
The burglars are so thin they worm up
rubbish chutes. Silent as cockroach.
The girls like European men for their size
and the colour of their skin.
They walk beneath umbrellas, etiolate
in air-conditioned rooms, dressed for cocktails.
They make perfect wives.

I'm nutmeg brown. I smoke Indonesian
cigarettes. I taste of cloves. Yes, I will visit
soon, in the golden flesh, I promise.

England in June: I have lungs again,
skin that fits, stalked nipples.
I move with sprung rhythm, finger the lives
of friends, laze in overgrown gardens.
I'm amazed at the delicacy of a dog-rose,
buttercups' spilt gold.
Tell me, was the sky always this wide?

I queue for the Summer Exhibition.
A girl is playing a violin, the notes so pure,
I weep. At the British Museum I dream
with Utamaro's girl: three aubergines,
two hawks and in the smoke blue distance
Mount Fuji burning.

An Inter-city nomad: north to south,
east to west. It's foxgloves I remember,
ten feet high and the way lanes twist and twist
careless between fields.

On a train to Colombo we are stacked
like cattle. Sweat runs into my eyes,
trickles, warm as urine, down my legs.
The women have sad eyes.
I sit on the floor, cross-legged, wheels
jarring my bones, watching
between the alpha legs of a man
at the open door – the bold red sun
bouncing on the sea's edge. At Polonnaruwa
I was as high as the feet of the sleeping Buddha.

The 125 glides through green waves.
Believe me, idyllic tropical islands
do not exist. I've seen them all.
Strips of blistering talcum sand fringing jungle.

Once, I crept inside. At first, nothing except

the unnerving shrill of cicadas and deep dark

dripping heat. Then I saw a twelve foot iguana

lumbering through fallen trees

and tangled lianas.

La recherche du temps perdu. There are things

I haven't told you, things I've almost forgotten.

The emerald sea's everything Cousteau dreamed up.

Everything. *Keep your eyes wide!* The purple eye

of a sea urchin is following me. It flexes

its wavy fronds as I pass. Strikes. The boatman

hammers the pain with a piece of rock.

Later, I lie flat on my back burning.

He applies fresh lime. Hammers again.

Travel does not necessarily broaden

the mind. There are tea-leaves between the pages

of my books. I'm packing sweaters. Ignore all rumours.

I'm having withdrawal symptoms for mountains.

I'm adjusting the strings of my parachute.

Jewelled Teardrop set in the Indian Ocean

Determined to escape from the shopping and eating scenario in Singapore, I was rescued by an out-of-the-blue invitation to spend Christmas with Patrick, an expatriate friend, at his home in Sri Lanka. It was 1987, a time when the upsurge in violence from the Tamil Tigers included shootings in Colombo and massacres of families in outlying villages. In spite of this, I didn't hesitate in accepting Patrick's offer. There were seven passengers on the flight to Colombo – six Sri Lankans and me – untimely confirmation of the possible dangers in store. Closing my eyes I succumbed to images of sky-reaching pagodas and meditating Buddhas and drifted towards sleep; then, as the aircraft began to lose height I looked down on the emerging coastline of the *jewelled teardrop set in the Indian Ocean –* as the island's former name of Ceylon, given by ancient mariners, was known.

No sooner had I touched down at Colombo airport than I was swiftly ushered into a black Mercedes limousine and driven in style, through the shabby back streets of the suburbs of Borello, to one of a number of haphazardly-styled but opulent houses. With afterthought extensions, tilting rooftops and gardens bursting with colour each was a celebration of its individuality. Such was the character of Patrick's abode: a delightful and convenient base from which to plan and set off on my travels.

The following morning, before the sun squinted over the rooftops, the houseboy served breakfast on the wooden balcony: pineapple, papaya, yoghurt, toast and honey, squares of butter floating on iced water and a bottomless pot of coffee. The air was scented with eucalyptus, frangipani and jasmine. Humming-birds beaded telegraph wires or hovered over waxy blooms. They scattered as several raucous crows swooped out of the sky and settled on neighbouring rooftops. From their vantage point they watched over the betel-spattered road like patient undertakers, as if they could smell death.

Kandy – former stronghold of Sinhalese kings

Rich in its ancient traditional culture of Buddhism – nestling in the foothills of the Hill Country – Kandy was first on my itinerary. Patrick warned against my inclination of hiring a driver and car and taking the uphill route by a road that winds round the sides of forested hills, obscuring picturesque views. Instead he recommended the more direct route by steam train, insisting that 'it offers splendid views and comparative comfort and takes less than three hours from Colombo.'

In fact, the Victorian train was in remarkably good shape; complete with wood panelling, burgundy leather seats – sagging but intact – and ornate gas lamps it was evocative of days of the Raj. There was even a buffet service. Tea, Indian style comes in an unusual range of colours varying from brick-dust red to chalky orange. When excessively thirsty I can ignore the colour but not the accompanying sweetness – usually from generous dollops of condensed milk. Today, I was in luck. My tea was pale grey and my emphatic pleas for no sugar had worked.

I had one side of the carriage to myself. On the opposite side a huddle of girls whispered together intently. The nearest, who had been giving me furtive glances, caught my eye and her face broke into a toothpaste smile. We chugged through shanty suburbs, across fields of rice-paddy draped in early mist, the sun's pale head nodding between rows of palms. A flock of tiny yellow birds blossomed and moved like a wave catching and shedding sunlight. Two girls emerged from a shack, immaculate and elegant, in emerald and purple saris. Rice fields gave way to plantations of coconuts and bananas which, in turn, merged into tropical forest. The dense growth, broken by occasional streams, crowded the track.

A sharp increase in gradient was marked by thinning trees and the engine's laboured progress. Open grassy slopes became rocky terrain. The now breathless engine almost came to a standstill. At one moment I feared we would slip backwards, topple into a river of scree and plunge down the precipitous slope. Then with a jerk, the engine recovered and we galloped along a ledge cut into a fortress of rock.

Seconds later, whistle blowing we raced into a tunnel. In thick darkness the magnified clacking of wheels and screeching whistle reverberated from the walls like the cries of the damned in Dante's *Inferno*. Wreathed in smoke we hurtled into sunlight. On one side the wall of rock leaned over us. On the other it fell away so that we were looking down a black precipice that fell to the tree-line. The train clattered and rattled as if it would fall apart. Now I understood why Patrick had advised me to take an inside seat. I resolved to do this on the downhill journey when the increase in speed was said to be so dramatic that one hour was cut from the uphill route.

I had booked a room at a guest house set into the hillside and within easy walking distance of the city, the lake and the renowned Temple of the Tooth. Small, unpretentious and charming it was open-plan and cooled by huge whirling fans. Flowers adorned every room filling the house with exotic perfume and colour. Windows from my room overlooked a swimming pool, gardens bordered by flowering shrubs and lawns sweeping to a fringe of trees; where the gardens ended tropical forest began. Monkeys played happy families in the trees and gave chase over the lawns.

Inside, a ceiling fan stirred the smell of must and the fumes of glowing moon-tigers – green coils that slowly burn throughout the night, repelling mosquitoes. A bell-shaped mosquito net, tied with an elaborate pink bow and resembling the voluminous skirt of a ball gown, swayed over the bed. I didn't have long to wonder about the necessity for the candles and matches on the bedside table. Just as it was growing dark the ceiling fan clicked to a halt. Within seconds sauna conditions, kept at bay by the fans, re-established themselves. Coils of smoke from moon-tigers grew into feathery plumes.

On the verandah, a waiter was lighting candles and setting my table for dinner. It looked and, for a short time, seemed romantic. This effect quickly wore off. As heat and humidity increased an invasion of mosquitoes took advantage of the situation and helped themselves to my blood. Without electricity the kitchens were out of action and the menu for dinner reduced to a choice of sandwiches. I retreated under the folds of my mosquito-netted bed to indulge in chicken and salad sandwiches accompanied by dry white wine.

It was while I was exploring Kandy that I discovered the distinct disadvantage of being fair, female and unaccompanied: a target for beggars, touts and easy prey for loitering, predatory males. I was walking through the main street trying to shake off a leech-like pursuer. Variations of 'Go away!' no matter how offensively or aggressively delivered seemed to keep him hanging on. In desperation I found myself looking round for support: a white face or a crocodile of tourists to get lost among. Then I heard my voice addressing my pursuer.

'I have to meet my husband at Queen's Hotel. I'm late,' I added, pointing at the white and imposing colonial building across the street. The effect was remarkable – as if I'd just sprayed him with insect repellent. I hurriedly crossed the road to the hotel making a mental note to adopt this strategy for survival in the future.

Refreshed and recharged from coffee in comfortable surrounds I emerged from the inner sanctum of the Queen's Hotel and headed for the inner sanctum of the renowned *Dalada Maligawa:* Temple of the Tooth. Housed in a complex of moated pink buildings that cluster along the shore of Kandy Lake, it was not difficult to locate. Named the Royal Palace Complex it included both the former King's and Queen's residences.

Following the directions of a sarong clad guide I entered the Hall of Beatific Vision where the revered tooth relic of Lord Buddha is contained in the smallest and innermost of seven interlocking caskets; made from pure gold each casket is engraved and ornamented with precious gems. Four elephant tusks stand guard over the outer casket: the great dagoba-shaped *karanduwa* – a gold plated reliquary, displayed on a silver table – was safeguarded by gilt railings.

My attention was taken by an embroidered wall hanging draped above the relic. A copy of a magnificent wall mural which hangs in the monastery of Kelaniya it illustrates the arrival in Sri Lanka of Prince Dantha and the Princess Hemamali. According to an ancient legend, the Buddha's tooth was taken from his body as he lay on a funeral pyre and smuggled to Sri Lanka in the 4th century AD; hidden in the hair of the princess, who was fleeing the Hindu armies besieging her father's kingdom in India, it arrived safely and has remained Sri Lanka's most prized possession ever since.

For the remainder of my stay in Kandy I decided to hire a driver-cum-guide. This usually guarantees personal safety, minimises hassle and allows for free choice of venues and the amount of time to be spent at each. Even if tour guides had been available I prefer chatting to a local driver speaking Pidgin English, than listening to a tour guide churning out potted history that I can read for myself.

The hotel staff soon had me sorted; comfortably seated in the back of a Range Rover I was en route through leafy tea-plantations to the Botanical Gardens. Girls in bright saris were splashes of colour among neat rows of green while in the distance magnificent views across ridge upon ridge of hills, ranging from shades of purple to blue and dusky grey, melted into the horizon. The zig-zag downhill route took us to the valley where the gardens border the Mahaweli River – more spacious and far cooler than those of Singapore. At this point I decided to accept an invitation from Yvan, the diver, for extensive viewing from a mule-driven cart.

Setting off along a shady avenue of palms – the river glinting between the fronds of bamboo – I imagined the aroma of coffee and cinnamon with which the tea gardens were originally planted. Then as we turned to cross open lawns Yvan pointed into the upper branches of a group of trees. At first I could make out nothing but leafy patterns. Then I saw them – larger versions of D.H. Lawrence's *'Creatures that hang themselves up like an old rag'* – not bats but flying foxes – *'grinning in their sleep'*.

We left the gardens but stayed with the river. At one point Yvan stopped and led me through trees to a steep cliff face. At the foot of a vertical drop of some 40 feet, the river – as wide as a dual carriageway – floundered round huge rock boulders. On the opposite side, surrounded by magnificent trees and thick foliage, the low bank curved in a wide arc. Yvan proudly informed me that the film *Tarzan* had been made at this spot. It was a perfect setting and I could well imagine Johnny Weissmuller yodelling and swinging from limb-thick lianas to rescue his Jane stranded mid-stream on a boulder.

'You like ride elephant?' Yvan asked as we made our way back to the cart.

'Yes,' was my spontaneous response. 'Yes, I'd love to.'

'First wash then ride.' Yvan replied, before explaining that in the heat of the afternoon, after a morning's work, the mahouts bring the elephants to the river to cool off and for their daily bath.

We followed a footpath to the river where several elephants were gathered. One, lying on its side, was half submerged in water. Instructed to remove my shoes I was then guided to stand close to the recumbent elephant. 'Round and round,' were the further instructions from the mahout as he handed me a brush. It was difficult to know where to begin on the huge mound before me and when I did there was no visible response from the recipient as I obediently made circular movements over its leathery belly. He appeared to be either in a state of static bliss or dead. Then, in answer to the mahout's encouraging voice, he struggled to his feet and it was time for my reward: a bare-back ride along a jungle path on the resurrected elephant. Hoisted onto his back, feet dangling and holding onto a rope tied round its neck, I felt more like Mowgli than a Maharaja.

The Ancient Walled City of Galle

Impressed by the success of my independent trip to Kandy my host suggested a further rail experience – this time to the ancient walled city of Galle. With its UNESCO world heritage Dutch fort complete with great ramparts, massive bastions and pepper pot towers and a wealth of other remains from its Dutch colonial heritage I was easily persuaded. I set about repacking my travel bag and lulled into

27

complacency by my trip to Kandy arrived at Colombo Station expecting a similar leisurely scenario. Shock at being confronted by a seething mass of bodies turned into panic. I wanted to leave but before I could retrace my steps to see if my lift was still in the forecourt a wiry male, claiming to be a porter, snatched my bag from my hand and promising to get me a seat when the train arrived, melted into the throng. I've never been good at scrums and still in a state of semi-shock I didn't resist. A thundering noise announced the train's arrival.

Before it had shunted to a standstill the entire body of fellow passengers advanced in an amorphous mass, surging through windows and doors. It was soon clear that not only were there no seats but there was no standing room either. What is more the porter had disappeared with my luggage and I was being propelled forward with the remaining crowd. It was a matter of going with them or being trampled underfoot. Miraculously, I recovered my bag and since there were no seats to save I paid the porter for his agility. As the train jolted into action I watched him expertly wriggle his way through a window back to the platform.

I was standing or propped somewhere in the middle of a carriage, bag between my feet and with nothing to hang on to. I couldn't tell where I began or ended, if the jutting bones belonged to me or my neighbours. The carriage was steaming like a laundry and the smell of sweat and spices overpowering. Some passengers were unwrapping parcels of curried rice and displaying a technique for eating, in such conditions, as an art form. By holding the package near to the face with one hand, and deftly flexing the wrist of the other it was possible to move fingers from rice to mouth and back in an oiled, hinge-like movement requiring the minimum of space. I watched fascinated until, once again, I became conscious of nothing but my own discomfort.

Heat escaping from my body in rivulets of sweat was trickling down crevices while the combined heat from the packed bodies was raising the temperature and humidity to beyond my level of endurance. I entered a type of self-induced coma. It was rather like having a fever when you surface from time to time feeling wretched but knowing there's nothing you can do until it passes. Apart from occasional glimpses of sea and palm trees I remember little of what I saw or thought for the next two hours. From time to time the train stopped. Nobody got off but vendors, selling canned drinks and more packets of rice, clambered on, over and between bodies. I've never felt more in need of a drink but my purse was squashed in my bag between my feet, out of sight and out of reach.

When we finally pulled into Galle Station the train emptied like a football stadium after a match and I found myself alone on the platform. Before I had limped into bright sunlight I was surrounded by voices:

'Taxi! You want hotel? You want taxi?'

'Yes, New Oriental,' I replied reciting the name recommended by Patrick. Grabbing hold of one handle of my bag, one of the men led me to a car that looked as if it had a worse experience than I had. I slumped onto the back seat nursing my bag. The driver got in the front door, two friends got in the other. The one in the middle arranged himself over the gear stick and handbrake. The vehicle jumped into gear, the engine juddered into a roar and we moved off in a cloud of blue fumes on what, after a few minutes, appeared to be a sightseeing tour of the backstreets of Galle. I knew that the hotel was just a few minutes from the station.

'New Oriental Hotel,' I reminded the driver.

'Sorry,' he said. 'Cannot – Tamil Tigers here this morning – police stop us – cannot. I take you to friend, very nice room, very cheap.'

'No!' I insisted, resorting to my survival strategy.

'I'm meeting my husband at the New Oriental. Take me there!'

'Cannot,' he repeated. 'Dangerous. See!' he added pointing to holes in the road. 'Tamil Tigers.'

This conversation was repeated with some syntactical variations and with all three men joining in from time to time. I was going through various stages of panic. Were they Tamil Tigers? Were they taking me hostage? Should I hurl myself from the car? That wouldn't work – at best I'd break a limb – at worst my neck – and they could stop and get me. The next stage was resignation. What could I do? A sort of numbness overtook me. This is it, I decided.

The man in the passenger window seat had turned round and was watching my face. Anger replaced numbness.

'Take me to the New Oriental Hotel, immediately. My husband is waiting. He'll send the police to look for me.'

There was some muttering between the front seats then, miraculously, a few moments later we were following the coast road, made a left-hand turn and drew alongside a set of white steps leading to the imposing colonnaded entrance of the hotel. A wave of relief flooded through me. Without any doubt that was one of my nine lives saved.

Built by the Dutch in 1684, the hotel appeared to be neither new nor oriental but it was a quiet, cool haven. A huge dining hall occupied the greater part of the ground floor. Wide sweeping staircases led to corridors in the upper level. A smell of beeswax drifted from dark polished woodwork and floors. As I signed in and was handed a cool hibiscus drink I decided that, more than any place

I've travelled to, the facility of moving in minutes from heaven to hell and back is nowhere more apparent than in Sri Lanka. The Land of *Serendib*[1] was living up to its reputation.

My room housed two queen-size four-poster beds, draped in muslin-mosquito-net curtains, a spacious lounge area and a writing desk. There was a large window at the far end but the moment I appeared a group of vendors, squatting below in the shade of a casuarina tree, were on their feet waving pieces of lace and a full-size lace tablecloth. I backed away closing the shutters.

Partial recovery was achieved after taking a bath in a tub large enough to hold a family of six, followed by a family-sized pot of tea. Full recovery was achieved at sundown; gin and tonic in my hand, ice clinking against the glass, I made my way from a stone balcony down a set of steps to the side of a sunken swimming pool, surrounded by banks of flowers. In evanescent light the colours of flowers, blossoming shrubs and trees deepened losing detail. Swallows dipped over the water. A possum shuffled by – just inches from my feet. The colour of my drink became a translucent blue – a reflection of the deeper tones of the pool. Overhead the great dome of sky released its stars.

The following morning my plan was to photograph parts of the remains of the Dutch Fort, the lighthouse, built in 1939 to replace the original 1848 light station that was destroyed by fire and some of the well-preserved Dutch buildings, especially Groote Kerk; built in 1755 it is the oldest protestant church still in use in Sri Lanka. Assured, by hotel staff, that it was possible to walk round the ramparts of the walled city of Galle in a morning and that I would not need a guide, I squared my shoulders and set off on foot. In harsh sunlight the buildings were a startling white. In an effort to reduce

---

[1] Land of unexpected discoveries & chances

the glare I attempted angled shots with my camera. Where the remains of the wall followed the sea-cliff I looked down on surf fishermen and bent figures washing their clothes in rock pools left by the tide. Before long, the combination of increasing heat and a non-stop stream of pursuing males drove me towards the market and, in spite of yesterday's experience, in search of a taxi.

To some extent the taxi ride was an action replay: the driver plus two friends in the front and reluctance to take me to the destination of my choice. This time, fortified by experience, I sat firmly on my imagination; believing that offers of cheaper accommodation with friends was purely in the interest of lining their pockets and unconnected with the ulterior motives of Tamil Tigers, I remained calm and collected, if not cool. Even when they discovered that I lived in Singapore and tried to persuade me to go home with them to meet a friend who had contacts in Singapore, I adopted a nonchalant manner and remained adamant and unmoved.

Finally, when I insisted that I had an appointment at the Closenberg Guest House and must be there by 12 noon but I'd like them to take me to the station later that day they deferred and agreed to come to the guest house at three p.m. to pick me up. This arrangement gave me time for lunch and fortification before the train journey back to Colombo and they benefited from the promise of another fare.

I wanted to visit the Closenberg as much for its historic past as for its up-market present. Formerly the home of a Dutch shipping-line captain, it was built in an idyllic position on a spit of land overlooking the lovely Closenberg Bay. Apart from a cement factory across the water the setting and views, from a stone white balustrade, overlooked dazzling turquoise sea on three sides.

'Hi! Did you come by yacht?' greeted a middle-aged man with a strong American accent. When I replied that I had come by train he lost interest and retreated to the bar. I ordered a long thirst-quenching lager and lime with plenty of ice, a seafood baguette and found a shaded spot on the flower-decked terrace to absorb the view. Modern yachts bobbed in the harbour: one, no doubt, belonged to the American. They were a far cry from the sea vessels of early traders blown into the ancient port by the Trade Winds; the same winds that acted as a shuttle service for Persians, Romans, Greeks, Arabs and Chinese who came and saw and conquered prizes of gold, silver, ivory, apes and peacocks. Malays and Indians, too, were visiting traders.

I tucked into my baguette, ordered coffee and leafed through my folder of notes. According to Sir James Emerson Tennent – Colonial Secretary of Ceylon (1845-1850) – Galle was the ancient seaport of Tarshish, from which King Solomon drew ivory, peacocks and other valuables. Certainly, cinnamon was exported from Sri Lanka as early as 1400 BC and since the root of the word Galle is Hebrew, it may have been the main port for the trade in spice. I was especially intrigued by references to discoveries of stone anchors of Indo-Arabian pattern in the ancient harbour; one weighing almost a ton (implying a ship of some size) and estimated to be around five hundred years old is thought to have its origins in Oman. Other finds include an anchor of Mediterranean pattern, similar to those used in Roman times and a celadon bowl of the Southern Song Dynasty (C13th) – one of the few relics of early trade with China. Today, yachts bobbed on sparkling waves with no hint of the fierce tides and storms that made the great harbour walls as much a necessity for past traders as they are for today's sailors.

Staff at the Closenberg organised a conventional taxi ride back to the hotel. I emerged at three p.m. to find my less conventional, pre-arranged lift to the station ready and waiting. The train was just as packed on the return journey to Colombo but on this occasion I knew what to expect and became agile and resourceful. Somehow I managed to forge a passage through steaming bodies to a space between the carriages, settled myself cross-legged on the floor, back to a wall, and immersed myself in Iris Murdoch's *Nuns and Soldiers*. When I tired of reading I had an excellent view of the sea through the legs of a man standing, feet apart, at the open door. As the sun dropped it became a swollen crimson ball bouncing along the sea's edge. Its equally red reflection bounced along the wet sand until both were swallowed and dissolved in blood red water.

The Golden Triangle

Anuradhapura, Polonnaruwa and Sigiriya: names to fire the imagination. Centuries before the birth of Christ, while the Greek Empire was flourishing in the Mediterranean and other regions still emerging from the late Stone Age the royal cities of the Sri Lanka's Golden Triangle were prosperous centres of trade.

On a pre-Christmas social evening in Colombo, arranged by my host, I was introduced to Hans and Martha, a resident Dutch couple, who invited me to join them on a tour of these ancient Buddhist settlements: a Christmas gift beyond all expectations. And so it was that early on the morning of Christmas Eve we left Colombo for the start of a three hour uphill drive along a road shrouded with dense jungle to a guest house on the very doorstep of Anuradhapura. After just under two hours of winding uphill, when the effect of views obscured by impenetrable trees was becoming strangely enervating, a road-side invitation to stop for coffee was greeted with unanimous approval.

A few minutes later we rounded a bend and turned onto a track that led to a weather-beaten wooden house in a clearing. There were some rickety cane chairs and a table in a porch at the front. The owner, a lugubrious looking man with a moth-eaten moustache and wearing a grubby T-shirt, tucked into a sarong, took our orders. When it came, the coffee was a dubious shade of khaki but the need for caffeine overrode caution; however, both the taste and smell more than lived up to expectations. Two mangy peacocks scratched at the baked earth on the remains of a lawn. The air was heavy with humidity. Then a slight breeze stirred the leaves of surrounding trees sending a chorus of cicadas into a frenzied maniacal screeching until reaching a crescendo in a unified single note, the screeching stopped as suddenly as it had started.

A few miles before we reached Anuradhapura – on the main route that branched north and east to the Tamil Tiger strongholds of Jaffna and Trincomalee – we were stopped at a road-block. It transpired that the Tigers had blown up the nearby railway tracks so road was the only public access to these regions. Armed, but lethargic soldiers took their time flicking through our passports before waving us on.

Just two years before our visit, the Tamil Tigers unleashed a ferocious attack in Anuradhapura; hijacking a bus they indiscriminately opened fire on innocent men, women and children before driving to the Buddhist Sri Maha Bodhi shrine and gunning down nuns, monks and civilians as they knelt in prayer. Memories of the incident, designed to provoke massive retaliation by the Sinhalese majority against the Tamils – in order to strengthen their position among the Tamil people – continued to fill local people and visitors with fear. My nervousness, from the road-side check point, defused as the distance between us increased. It was a relief when announcing the journey's end Hans turned the vehicle into an avenue lined by spiky shrubs; like patrols of angry porcupines they guarded the entrance to the rest house.

Guest rooms, in a small block separate from the main building, opened onto a shared verandah elegantly furnished with rattan chairs and tables. Inside my room a ceiling fan stirred the smell of must and sent a bell-shaped mosquito net swaying over the bed. Closeness to

Tamil Tiger strongholds meant that no more than a trickle of visitors reached these historic regions; hotels and rest houses were largely empty and unused. On Christmas evening we were the only visitors.

After the journey, ablutions were first on the itinerary. Keeping my eyes fixed on a large cockroach skulking under the wash basin I took a shower and planned to get help to eject it. By the time we had refreshed ourselves and evicted the intruder a waiter was crossing the lawn with a tray of iced drinks. The garden stretched before us – a profusion of flowers, shrubs and trees decorated with multitudes of butterflies of every shape and colour, some the size of small birds. There was an incredible ambience – whether it was nearness to the ancient ruins or the place itself it was impossible to tell but the aura was magical.

The following morning my companions suggested that we should hire bicycles to explore the remains of the nearby Buddhist site. The proposition made me extremely nervous. I hadn't ridden a bicycle for a good many years and my tall and lean companions looked super-fit. Hans had changed into shorts and a sports shirt which stretched over well-defined chest and arm muscles and Martha was similarly equipped and attired. I had a vision of ending up either in a ditch or watching them disappear over a brow of a hill as I struggled to push my bike to the top. But now it was too late to withdraw. Maps in pockets we set off scrunching down the gravel drive and generating our own refreshing breeze.

Minutes later we were crossing the road bridging the Malavathu Oya River where fully dressed locals, standing waist-deep in water, were soaping themselves and their clothes in a froth of bubbles; we followed a tree-lined tarmac path that was once part of a sophisticated network of roads linking the original 20 square mile settlement. On either side, the plain was littered with ancient ruins: the remains of vast dagobas, monasteries, shrines, lecture halls and landscaped gardens. The easy gradient of our ride and the thought-provoking nature of our surroundings soon overcame my fear of lack of fitness. Each time we stopped we were immersed in an absolute stillness. I imagined the swishing of robes as barefooted monks walked between avenues of trees deep in contemplation.

In its time, Anuradhapura was the greatest city in Sri Lanka and home of the legendary forefathers of the Sinhalese race. In the 10th Century AD, at the height of its glory, the civilization spread from the Tiber to the Yellow Sea. The king lived in a bejewelled palace of 1,000 chambers; gold pinnacled shrines rose hundreds of feet into the air. Even today, second only to the Pyramids of Egypt in size and splendour, its ruins continue to feed the imagination.

The most impressive monuments, at least for their size, are the dagobas – great Buddhist commemorative sites or stupas. The largest, Jetavanaramaya – 500 feet high and 370 feet in diameter – covering eight acres of land is reputed to be larger than all but two of the pyramids. Sadly centuries of weathering have taken their toll on the red, outer brick wall which has disintegrated; grass and shrubs have taken root giving the appearance of little more than a symmetrical hill. By contrast the white bell-shaped dagobas remained aesthetically pleasing, especially those crowned by a white octagonal pillar and topped by a spire.

Boasting an impressive spire and surrounded by a huge courtyard with fortified walls decorated with a circle of black elephants Ruwanweli Seya – one of the most impressive dagobas – had our cameras clicking and whirring. In line with Buddhist cosmology which decrees that elephants uphold the earth these elephants are said to be upholding the dagoba. But there is more to the dagobas than meets the eye. Like the pyramids they are storehouses of ancient treasures built to outlast man: holy relics, paintings and sculptures are said to remain buried, hidden from the human eye. Standing before Ruwanweli Seya – the Great Stupa – reminded me of Samuel

Johnson's description of the philosopher Imlac when he takes Rasselas to gaze upon the pyramids. He could just as easily have been describing the dagobas when he tells Rasselas:

It seems to have been erected only in compliance with that hunger of imagination which preys incessantly upon life...

For an uplifting spiritual experience we decided to head for the ancient papal tree – believed to have originally been grown from a branch of the Bodhi Tree at Bodh Gaya (Bihar, India), under which Gautama Buddha attained Enlightenment. In the 3rd century BC the emperor Asoka sent a cutting from the sacred tree for the newly converted Buddhists in Sri Lanka. Said to have been planted in Anuradhapura about 245 BC it is reputed to be the oldest tree in existence for which there is a historical record. Standing on a platform, encircled by a gold plated railing, branches of the ancient tree are now supported by iron crutches. The spiral shaped leaves, believed to have influenced the shape of the dagobas, provided welcome contemplative shade. Alongside, were the remaining columns of a palace. It needed a powerful imagination to reconstruct the former building. Founded by King Dutugemunu (161-137 BC) the structure was once home to a community of 1,000 Buddhist monks whose duties included tending the sacred tree; the entire nine-storey building, once decorated with silver and gems and sheltered by a bronze roof, was originally supported by 1600 pillars. Now, the columns are all that remain. The rustling of a lizard through long grass was the only sound to disturb the heavy silence.

Minutes later, attracted by the elaborately carved walls of a monastery we stopped to explore. At first we thought the building was just a shell and apart from the walls nothing of real interest remained. Then as I approached the front wall, at the foot of a flight of steps, I caught sight of a remarkable intact moonstone marking the entrance to the former monastery. A lotus petal representing male and female creative forces held centre stage. Surrounding this were concentric bands of creatures symbolising the perils of life: elephants – birth; horses – death and geese – the distinction between good and evil. When the monks entered the monastery the act of crossing the moonstone symbolised transcendence over worldly temptation and led to the achievement of wisdom and insight. Considering the hundreds of soft-footed monks who must have crossed the moonstone, its state of completeness was both a pleasure and a surprise.

*****

After breakfast on Christmas morning we decided to explore the remains of the Royal Pleasure Gardens which lie beyond the bund of Tissa Wewa, one of two huge irrigation lakes which flank Anuradhapura and, amazingly, formed the basis of an impressive irrigation network dating from the 3rd Century BC. The gardens, covering 400 acres, are strewn with massive rock boulders, many of which were once capped by summer houses. Today, after centuries of exposure to sun, wind and rain they are impressive natural monuments. I climbed to the top of one. Its natural rock hollows, as smooth as marble, were filled with water from last night's rain. The air was sweet and cool. From the top I looked down on well-drained gardens: avenues of trees, lawns, flowerbeds and a group of three adjacent ponds separated by rectangular tiered walls but linked by a flight of steps. The water mirrored cobalt blue sky; reflections of the tops of cumulus trees floated like heavy-headed flowers.

Once again I was conscious of an incredible stillness, accentuated by my elevated position and solitude. This time it did not evoke the swishing of monks' robes but filled me with nostalgia. It was my first Christmas away from my family and I found myself imagining and even willing their presence. At that moment I heard children's voices and then I saw dark heads appearing over the curve of the boulder. Six children, clutching fistfuls of flowers, were scrambling to the top of the rock. The eldest, a girl of about 10 years, handed me her posy and greeted me with 'Happy Christmas'. A chorus of Happy Christmases followed as flowers were dropped into my lap. They sat around me in a circle, smiling. Tearful Madonna of the rock, with a lap full of flowers, I was surrounded by a family of dark-eyed children.

*****

The road to Sigiriya wound like a leafy Devon lane through fields of sugar-cane. Along one section we passed first one and then a succession of miniature houses on stilts. Each had a balcony on which a life-size effigy of a family, rather like well-dressed scarecrows, stood with outstretched arms. When we stopped to take photographs, a real family emerged from a field. One of the boys explained that the effigies had been erected to scare elephants from the crops. Apparently, the farmers have planted sugar-cane over the elephants' ancient route to their watering hole. The stilt houses are used as look-outs for sighting the elephants when they return to the route. Then members of the family join the figures on the balcony and bang tins together to frighten the elephants away.

As we approached Sigiriya, the great red, rock fortress could be seen rising 600 feet from an ocean of jungle. On the summit stands the remains of the palace of King Kasyapa whose cruelty and avarice for his father's fortune led him to have his father put to death by walling him alive within his tomb. Then fearing for his own safety he fled and had his palace built on the summit of Sigiriya Rock. From this splendid citadel he ruled and defended his kingdom for seven years.

There was a steady drizzle on the day of our visit which promised to make the climb over slippery rock treacherous. The approach, through landscaped gardens, had a gentle gradient. The real climb began at the foot of the massive rock-fortress, up a flight of steps between the gigantic sculptured paws of a lion. Originally, the final and most difficult part of the ascent was through the lion's open jaws. Today, only the paws remain. Above them a narrow passage leads uphill to a spiral staircase cut into the rock face and caged on the outside to prevent visitors from falling off the edge. This, in turn, leads to a sheltered grotto within a tunnel of rock where the remaining 22 frescoes of the Sigiriya maidens can still be seen. No-one knows if the beautiful bare-breasted maidens were the wives or concubines of Kasyapa or heavenly nymphs. Whatever their origin they were the high point of the climb.

Unsuitably shod and faced with the final part of the ascent over a steep, wet rock-face with nothing but a sagging rope to hang on to, I lost my nerve. I left the glories of the summit to my super-fit, suitably shod companions. Even from my vantage point it was obvious that Kasyapa's guards could not have had a more dramatic nor advantageous look-out from which to sight processions of elephants bearing warring enemies.

The Dambulla Cave Temple – built into the summit of a massive granite rock which rises 350 feet above Dambulla village – just a few miles from Sigiriya – guards the entrance to a series of five caverns renowned for their wall paintings and a number of sculptured Buddhas – 48 in all. Its history dates back to the 2nd Century BC when King Valagam Bahu, driven from Anuradhapura by invading enemies, took refuge in the caves.

It was a bright, clear morning when we began the ascent. The entire rock face has been cut into a series of steps and terraces requiring mechanical effort rather than climbing skills and, therefore, assailable even by me. From time to time overspreading trees cast welcome shade and provided a playground for monkeys. Some squatted on the steps picking at food scraps, sticky wrappers or grooming each other with pernickety gestures. On the terraces displays of postcards, slides, trinkets and miniature Buddhas were on sale to the straggle of visitors. The occasional saffron-robed monk glided by. During our leisurely ascent a fellow traveller confessed that he had lived as a Buddhist for several years in a village in Nepal. Finally, he had grown tired of the restraints: a daily bowl of self-grown rice and vegetables; sleeping on a straw mat on the mud floor and walking several miles each day to draw water from a well. When he left he threw himself into an Epicurean lifestyle to compensate for years of self-denial.

Inside the caves it was cool and dark requiring several moments to adjust from the heat and glare outside. The most interesting paintings in the fourth cavern covered walls and ceiling following the natural rock curves. Better preserved than Sigiriya's seductive maidens, the paintings were more in line with Buddhist aestheticism: saintly ascending figures; warriors brandishing spears and celebrating the triumph of good over evil and spherical trees and flowers in subtle tones of sepia, rose, and grey-blues. The overall effect was of weightlessness and tranquility rather like an underwater scene.

Other caverns were remarkable for replicated golden Buddhas. In the centre of one a white bell-shaped dagoba, capped by a golden spire, was circled by outward facing seated Buddhas. In another, rows of standing Buddhas lined the walls, arms bent from the elbows – the right hand of each in a position of benediction or protection: the circular and lineal repetition of images suggestive of continuity and timelessness.

*****

Our final visit was to the magnificent ruins of Polonnaruwa: the capital and centre of Buddhism after the conquest of Anuradhapura in the 11th century AD. There are many remarkable ruins in Polonnaruwa but the *pièce de résistance* must be the Gal Vihara (Rock Shrine): four magnificent mid-12th century statues carved from a single wall of granite.

It was a day of white heat: translucent lines shimmered like bent glass over the parched grass of the vast arena which held the shrine. On one side was the great wall of carved rock and on the other, some fifty metres distant, a granite hill provided natural viewing points from which all four Buddhas could be seen. I climbed the hill until I was in a fairly central position. Opposite me was the 23 foot high standing Buddha, his arms crossed in a relaxed attitude. On his left two seated Buddhas adopted the traditional lotus position of deep meditation. Finally, on the right was the magnificent and colossal recumbent Buddha stretching 46 feet from head to foot and depicted at the moment of physical death and transcendence to *parinibbana* – the liberation from the repeated cycle of birth, life and death for which every Buddhist strives. This enlightened state is suggested by the position of his toes which are held slightly apart. Held together they represent no more than a reclining attitude. Close-up, I was the same height as the Buddha's feet: a splendid and fitting image to end the exploration of The Golden Triangle and my visit to the *jewelled teardrop in the Indian Ocean.*

A Houseboat in Kashmir

Kashmir in November: temperatures below freezing. Would I survive after two blood-thinning years in the Tropics? These were my thoughts on the last lap of the journey from Singapore to Srinagar; ears signalling descent I looked down to see the breathtaking view of a range of mountains growing beneath me: the Himalayas dusted with snow. The aircraft circled and dropped into a wide valley plain, renowned in summer for abundant supplies of flowers, fruit and vegetables. Now, with winter fast approaching, it was a uniform bronze in late sunlight.

A huge red banner celebrating forty years of freedom from British rule greeted me as I walked across the tarmac of Srinagar Airport. Suddenly, I was aware that I was the only obvious British passenger. I have never considered myself overtly patriotic. In fact, I have chosen to live as an expatriate and have more than a healthy inbuilt cynicism for patriotic fervour but there is something about believing you are the sole representative of a race on alien soil and feeling threatened – no matter how impersonal – that stirs even muddy patriotic sentiment. I was overcome by a feeling of responsibility for not only supporting the Union Jack but for the entire creaking history of the British Empire.

Sentiments were quickly lost as I struggled past armed soldiers, through various controls, form-filling and luggage retrieval to be met by the customary bombardment of touts, would-be taxi drivers, taxi-drivers, brothers and friends of taxi-drivers. I was relieved to be rescued by Yosuf, the son of the family who owned the houseboat I was to stay on, though a little unnerved to learn that the last houseboat visitor left two weeks previously and I was to be the only house-boat guest on Lake Nagin. However, there was nothing I could do except trust Yosuf's assurances that I would be perfectly safe since, he explained, his family home was just a few hundred metres from the boat. I wasn't sure how this would help in an emergency, in the middle of the night. Nevertheless, I turned down his suggestion that the houseboy should sleep on board with me. I wasn't that nervous.

The forty minute drive from the airport was through wide dusty streets lined with chinar trees still clinging to the last of their fiery, burnished leaves and an increasing number of large, rambling, detached houses all three storeys high. Similar in design to Patrick's house in Colombo – each had a distinguishing characteristic, usually in the particular shape and angle of the sloping roof or tip-tilted gables.

Yosuf explained that each family builds their own home and live as a community: parents, grandparents, uncles, cousins, aunts and children. They share the chores and cook the evening meal together. Unlike the expatriate homes in Colombo these large several storey houses are invariably unfinished, without glass in the windows and largely unfurnished apart from the customary luxury of Kashmir rugs and cushions on the floors. Cooking and heating are done by charcoal and during the snowed-in winter months each person keeps warm by carrying a woven basket holding a clay pot of burning charcoal under a loose cape-like coat. When seated on the floor the personal heating system is placed between crossed legs. By Western standards the people are poor but, Yosuf explained that in this predominantly Muslim community there is no abject poverty or homelessness as there is in many areas in India.

45

By the time we arrived the sun was low in the sky and the air distinctly frosty. A backdrop of shadowed mountains, appeared to both cradle and threaten the lake where the legendary house boats were tucked round the edges, under a fringe of willows. Inherited from the days of the Raj when, unable to own land, British residents made their homes in the hand carved house boats; the majority have three or even four bedrooms and today are rented by visiting families or friends who don't mind sharing. I had been inappropriately assigned the 'honeymoon' boat. It was the smallest. Every inch, inside and out is hand carved, the furnishings handmade and hand-woven and the floors fully carpeted. In the centre of the lounge, and in the bedroom, stood an ungainly but necessary iron wood burner. Hasan, my house boy, had the fires burning and I was served tea and cake – a warm and English welcome.

Hasan wasn't so much a house boy as a house man. He wouldn't see fifty again. His primary winter duty was to keep the fires burning. Most of the pieces of wood appeared to be either too long or too wide to fit in the container which meant that the lid didn't shut. Smoke, which escaped from the lid and the elbow-shaped metal chimney, belched into the room. Hasan was possessive about his fire duties and peeved if I 'interfered' – as was sometimes necessary when he wasn't there and the fire threatened to go out and I was in danger of frost-bite; or so much smoke was billowing into the room that I was in danger of asphyxiation.

Hasan's other important duty was to serve my meals which were prepared and cooked over an on-shore charcoal burner. Mutton and chicken were served alternately and were equally good when either stewed or curried. Problems arose when the cook decided to please my Western palate by grilling or roasting. The quality of the meat was such that no amount of chomping or attempts at chewing succeeded in reducing the texture of the pieces to a comfortable size to swallow. My only option was to drink mouthfuls of mineral water as a swallowing aid.

There was only one gastronomical disaster. I was presented with a bowl of liquid containing grey rubbery lumps. To my knowledge, I have never tasted sheep's balls but I was convinced that was what I was attempting to eat. It reminded me of early 'going ethnic' days in Singapore when I was served a similar concoction at a hawker stall. It was one of the few occasions when I have been ill after eating at a stall in Singapore. Later, I learned that the same stall holder had been prosecuted for advertising pig's penis soup raising an even more off-putting possibility. In true Singaporean-Chinese style he was allowed to serve it but not advertise it. The Chinese penchant for tiger's penis obviously does not stop there but, at least, pigs and sheep are not endangered species resulting from the gastronomical whims of the nation.

In addition to his wounded spaniel eyes, which made upsetting him by fiddling with the fire or not eating the food he had prepared difficult, there are two things I remember about Hasan: his feet and his English. His feet because they were bare and temperatures were below freezing. I decided that he must have grown Hobbit-like soles as he appeared impervious to the cold. His English was memorable from his impeccable enunciation which was far superior to that of even the most highly educated Singaporeans. A legacy from his education in an English mission school, it was a distinct advantage in his dealings with the steady flow of English speaking summer visitors.

There were many light-fittings on the boat but there was insufficient light to read or write by during the long dark evenings. At best there was a dull glow. Since electricity supplies relied entirely on water-power and by now mountain streams were no more than a trickle, adequate supplies of Duty Free were essential to help pass the longest and coldest nights I have ever experienced.

Following the sauna conditions of Singapore the shock to my system was maximised. Without constant attention the wood burners went out and although my bed was over weighted with blankets it felt damp. I could sense the iron-cold of the lake seeping through the timber and bedding into my bones. This, of course, explained why there were no other visitors. Although I discovered the door to the boat didn't lock I suffered no more than fleeting moments of fear evoked by creaking timbers or the night-cries of birds during my stay.

Waking before it was light with no prospect of a cup of tea until Hasan arrived was a severe test of character. There was nothing I could do except pull on my purple gloves, wind the matching scarf round my neck and go on deck to wait for morning to arrive. The wailing chant of the muezzin was the dawn chorus I longed for. Then, after adding even more layers of clothes than I had slept in, I crept into the icy bathroom to clean my teeth and splash my face with water. In the interests of survival personal hygiene was minimised for the next few days.

By the time I emerged grey light was thinning and mountains beginning to take shape. Surrounding willows and grasses were white and stiff with frost. Camera slung round my neck, fingers tucked under my armpits I waited on the terrace for the moment that was to be the reward for surviving the night: the huge red sun slipping over serrated mountain peaks surprising its reflection in the lake. This moment was a signal for birds to be on the move: sea-hawks, the size of small eagles; pied kingfishers and the more usual turquoise variety slicing the water; yellow breasted bull-bulls nodding their heads and beading the mooring ropes.

Then, silent as a dream, the first long-boat appeared from the layer of mist drifting across the lake. As morning progressed the mist dispersed and the traffic of boats increased. On return trips they were heaped with lotus leaves, flowers, fruit and vegetables for the markets. During the summer months the boat-people make a handsome living selling their goods and craft work to houseboat guests. A telegraph system seemed to have announced my arrival as one after the other boatmen appeared at the steps of my terrace. Engaging salesmen as they were, since I was the sole object of their persuasion, their persistence became tiring. I bought more gifts than I have friends to distribute them to: embroidered shawls, leather purses, flower seeds, *papier mache* ornaments and a beautiful silver ring in which a turquoise tourmaline stone was set. I was their last hope of cash before winter and they were not deterred by the growing ferocity of my refusals. My only resort was to shut myself in the boat and pretend I wasn't there.

Each morning after breakfast, Yosuf arrived to escort me on a trip or visit. We began with a tour of Srinagar. Once a walled city – today the hill fort and remains of the wall are crumbling monuments to the Mughal Emperor, Akbar; it is now a bustling market town and handicraft centre sprawling along the banks of the River Jhelum. River house-boats – miniature versions of the more luxurious lake house-boats – lived in by local people for centuries, line the river banks. One of the most attractive features – hand-made wooden roof-tiles – resembled overlapping leaves.

Activity in and around the boats had the air of a pre-winter spring clean: boats being scrubbed, washing pummelled, lengths of brightly coloured cloth flailed against rocks. Women were busy washing and making pots from heaps of wet clay. Men were busy enjoying the last of the sun – squatting by the roadside and smoking the traditional water-pipes known locally as hubbly bubblies. If I had stayed there long enough I could have got high on the aroma. On the distant curve of the river, through blue-grey mist, the spired dome of Jami Masjid Mosque conjured Persian Tales.

Away from the river we explored medieval streets: narrow bazaars shaded beneath overhanging gables; tiny cobbled alleys sneaking between timber-framed walls with triffid-like plants squeezing from crevices. We climbed a dark staircase hung with carpets to a brassware shop where, sitting cross-legged on the floor, I was served cinnamon and ginger tea from a porcelain tea-set. On learning that I was British the owner spent some time rummaging through drawers until he finally and proudly produced a signed photograph of Lord Mountbatten taken in this very shop.

The last British Viceroy of India and the first Governor General, at the time of Indian Independence in 1947, Lord Mountbatten's voice was instrumental in the decision to accede Jammu and Kashmir to India. Holding the signed photograph evoked a tangible sense of the past. Unable to persuade the Muslim leader Mohammed Ali Jinnah of the benefits of a united, independent India resulted in the partition of India and Pakistan – this in turn led to widespread inter-communal violence. In spite of this the love of British people for Kashmir and the warmth and friendship of the Kashmiri people to British visitors was wholly evident throughout my stay. This was confirmed on my next visit to a nearby store selling leather goods; a charming old man, of some six feet tall, insisted on standing in one of his bags while his assistant and I lifted it to demonstrate the quality of the leather and stitching. The bag passed the test. My shoulder ached for days.

Markets spilled across wider modern streets. Cattle and people wandered between stalls. Some of the older women wore black chadors, their eyes covered by black net grills. Others were completely westernised in their dress. An indication of further confusion and conflicts – this time over the late Shah's decree in which the *chador* and the *hijab* were abolished – followed by the late

Ayatollah Khomeini's reversal of this pronouncement. Muslim males, encountering no such problems, wandered about in various combinations of wrap-around drapes and trousers.

Carpets bloomed from hedges and fences. The most attractive and expensive are pure silk – the colours changing according to the direction of light. There are plenty of factory outlets for carpets where, in spite of costs for transportation, prices are considerably lower than shopping for the equivalent in Singapore or Harrods, though higher than those that can be bartered for with market-holders and tourist-wise boatmen.

The two hour drive to Gulmarg in the foothills of the Himalayas, along a straight road lined with poplars, reminded me of long tree-lined roads in France. But that is where the similarity ended. Patches of road were badly potholed and at the edges the tarmac surface petered out to deep ruts, stones and dust. Added to this was the utter chaos created by other road-users: sheep, cattle, horse-drawn carts, cars, lorries and people carrying assorted goods on their heads, all jockeying for position and survival.

Like fellow drivers, Yosuf kept his hand on the horn for most of the journey. This cacophony appeared to have little effect on the other road users but had a remarkable effect upon my throbbing head. Although accustomed to erratic and dangerous driving in Asia, the Srinagar 'cross-road experience' is without parallel. There was one rule. The fastest and most aggressive drivers took priority. It was Yosuf's skill and swerving, race-track style, that got us through. Somewhere, in the near middle, I saw a policeman blowing a whistle and waving his arms. He was ignored by all.

As we began the slow climb into the Himalayas the traffic thinned and the road cut between mile after mile of bronze terraced rice-fields, redundant until next summer's rain. Then a group of women appeared carrying huge bundles of firewood on their heads and moving at a slow trot to maintain their balance on the downhill path. I asked Yosuf to stop so that I could capture them on film. In spite of their heavy loads, they still managed to smile when I had to run backwards to get them in focus for a photograph. The road narrowed to a path and followed hairpin bends between dark pines to Gulmarg – known in summer as the 'meadow of flowers' and boasting the highest golf course in the world.

In winter it is transformed into a ski resort. Compared to European standards the facilities, equipment and runs would not satisfy the serious skier although the kudos of skiing in the Himalayas may well satisfy the ego. Now, it was a wide grassy bowl, the day bright and still and Nanga Parbat – the ninth highest mountain in the world – just visible through a gauze of mist. The only sounds were the occasional clatter of mountain ponies crossing the tarmac path and the thud of giant cones dropping.

Another disadvantage of the timing of my visit was that it was the wrong time of year for trekking, one of the major attractions of the region. I am not convinced that I would make a good trekker. I am easily distracted from the main route by anything that takes my interest – following a butterfly with my camera or clambering through dense undergrowth to get a better view. I was still keen to try but had been unable to find a guide willing to risk being marooned by impending snow.

One of the most enjoyable experiences of my visit was a ride in a *shikara* – a hand-paddled water-taxi – generously furnished with rugs and cushions. All I had to do was lie back and listen to the rhythm of the paddles scooping the water in the style of the '*Jewel in the Crown*'. This romantic aura quickly disappeared when, at my request, the boatman took me to photograph some older men who were digging up lotus roots in low-lying brackish water. We became lodged on a tree root and keeled dangerously to one side. I am not usually averse to swimming but the thought of being immersed in the freezing black water of the lake did not appeal. However, with some expert rocking from Yosuf, the near drama was averted and we set off again gliding towards the lake islands.

Local families live on these islands in houses as stylish and unfinished as those on shore. They earn their living by growing fruit and vegetables on 'floating islands' fashioned from bulrushes interwoven with mud. Once again the boatman was keen to demonstrate his prowess – on this occasion he insisted on standing on one of the islands to test its stability. His feet got wet but it was as buoyant as a raft. The lake and its reflections provided splendid opportunities for taking photographs and bird watching.

My last memory of Srinagar is of having to take a detour of the town to reach the airport. It was Friday and mid-day – the streets were paved with prayer mats and on each a figure was bent in an attitude of prayer. My lasting and treasured memory is of the immense silence encompassing the lake: not a breath of wind, silvery sunlight, a frost-held stillness, the tangible expectant silence before heavy snow. A voice, the cry of a bird magnified, echoing across the lake.

1947: The end of British rule in India and the partition of the subcontinent into mainly Hindu India and the Muslim majority of Pakistan led to ongoing outbreaks of violence over boundaries and frontiers and the ownership of Kashmir. Fortunately the timing of my visit – 1987 – was such that apart from armed soldiers at the airport on my arrival there were no obvious signs of the complex tensions leading to further violence and war in 1998 when Pakistani guerrillas established a reign of terror until 1999.

Island of Dreams

I first decided to visit Sabah while reading a promotion feature in a Malaysian airline magazine. At the time I was flying somewhere between the Langkawi Islands and Singapore when suddenly the sky became filled with turbulent cloud and the aircraft buffeted by wind and rain; passengers and staff were directed to be seated with belts fastened. It was either the end of the summer monsoon or the beginning of the winter monsoon.

It's always pre, during or post monsoon in Singapore. I spent the first few months waiting for it as if it were a distinct event, like the arrival of a bad-tempered monster that would wreak havoc and leave a trail of destruction in its wake. Finally, a few false starts were followed by days of torrential rain when the flooding was so bad that the storm drains couldn't cope, taxis weren't running and I couldn't get to work for several days. That over the weather settled into the diurnal pattern of high temperatures and humidity, interspersed with heavy downfalls of rain, accompanied by dramatic thunderclaps and lightning.

This gusty squall had deprived me of after-dinner coffee; even the cabin crew were confined to their seats. I pulled down the window blind and allowed myself to be seduced by the mysteries of 'Borneo's Paradise'. Safely back in my Singapore apartment, before I had brushed the sand from the Langkawi Islands from my feet, I was on the phone to my travel agent and Sabah was on the horizon.

Four months later, accompanied by my daughters, Catriona and Justine, we arrived in Kota Kinabalu, Sabah's capital. We were staying overnight while en route for the *Floating Hotel* in Semporna, recommended by David, a well-travelled Kiwi friend. At that time the area was visited by intrepid travellers and divers, attracted by the beauty of its untouched off-shore islands and coral reefs – in particular, Sipadan Island which caps a limestone pinnacle 20 miles offshore in the Celebes Sea. Famous for the underwater life found in and around its subterranean cliffs, caverns and reefs, Sipadan was also reputed to be regularly visited by dolphins and a favoured breeding ground for great green turtles. It was the island of our dreams. At that time Borneo Divers was the only diving unit operating on the then pristine island. It was the place we were intent on visiting. Before setting off I contacted Borneo Divers and the hotel to make arrangements for a boat to take us from Semporna to Sipadan.

The outline of Mount Kinabalu, South-East Asia's highest and most visited mountain, rising from a cluster of cloud, greeted us the following morning. Mount Kinabalu is to Sabah what Saint Peter's is to Rome – a sacred place which attracts an endless stream of pilgrims. The strenuous climb takes three days with overnight stops in simple rest huts for modern pilgrims. Since the greater part of the route has been converted into a natural staircase, made from tree roots and branches in the lower section and from steps hewn into the rocks in the upper region, the ascent is said to be more a test of endurance than climbing skills.

There are various stories accounting for the mountain's name. Some people believe it came from the legend told by local Kadazan people, that spirits of ghosts of the dead live on the summit; the Kadazan words *Aki Nabalu* – used to describe the mountain – translate as 'sacred place of the dead'. Others believe it came from a legend about a Chinese prince called *kina* meaning 'China' and *balu* meaning 'widow'. In this legend the prince climbed the mountain in search of a huge pearl which was hidden and guarded by a fierce dragon. The prince killed the dragon and stole the pearl. He then married a Kadazan maiden but soon left her and returned to China. His heart-broken wife went to the mountain where she was turned to stone. Whatever the origin of the name, Mount Kinabalu has been considered sacred from ancient times and a place of pilgrimage by the Kadazan people.

Today, the ancient trail attracts more sightseers than pilgrims. They come for the challenge of reaching the summit; to experience the spectacular changes in flora and fauna during the ascent and, if they time the final stage of the ascent accurately, to watch sunrise from the summit. Even long-distance, from our hotel, the sight of the mountain's pinnacles spiralling into blue sky was awe-inspiring but we had set our sights on magical underwater scenes.

The last stage of our journey was the one hour flight south to Tawau, followed by taking a taxi to Semporna – the nearest place in Sabah for reaching Sipadan Island. From the moment we arrived in Tawau it was evident that we were the only 'foreign' visitors. Experience rather than a suspicious nature had taught me it was time to be 'on guard'. New arrivals in unfamiliar surroundings and handling a strange currency are easy targets for those eager to make a profit. Nevertheless, our bags were snatched and we were propelled to one of a huddle of dilapidated cars serving as taxis. Despite language problems I managed to negotiate an acceptable fare for the estimated ninety minute drive to Semporna. This was confirmed in writing on the back of the driver's hand before we took off.

At first the undulating gravel track cut straight through jungle. It wasn't difficult to imagine local Murut headhunting tribes slipping between tangled lianas or our distant cousins, the orangutan, swinging over their heads, just metres from where we passed. Once we hit the pot-holed tarmac road there was little traffic and apart from the sudden, incongruous appearance of a crocodile of schoolchildren, neatly dressed in European-style uniforms, it was largely deserted.

Heat and humidity were intense. Catriona and Justine survived by pressing their faces into streams of hot air whipping through the window. Find it yourself air conditioning. Squashed between them and evaporating onto the plastic seat I clung to dreams of days of exploring coral reefs in turquoise sea.

All too soon reality replaced romantic imaginings. Sheltered by a large open-sided umbrella-shaped roof, the hotel – a wooden structure standing on six metre stilts in water as thick and brown as gravy – was flanked on one side by market stalls tumbling towards water littered with plastic bags, bottles and debris, and on the other side by the long-legged water houses of local fishermen. Fishing boats – carried by rectangular sails in indecisive wind – scurried to and fro. Behind the market the golden dome of a slender minaret, adjacent to a small white mosque, graced the skyline. Semporna, also known as 'Pearl City', once the centre of a flourishing trade based on the exchange of local pearls and tortoise-shell with the Chinese for silk and luxury goods, was dusty, noisy and ramshackle.

The sea was not turquoise but there was cold beer and time to take in our surroundings from the open-air bar and dining area. We consoled ourselves that we were in transit and it was just a matter of time until someone from Borneo Divers would arrive and take us to magical Sipadan Island and, as soon as there was a member of staff in the empty reception area, we would check arrangements for our departure.

Walkways radiated in the form of a fan from the dining area to the reception, guest rooms and a jetty. In the few minutes since our arrival pockets of curious locals had been gathering and were moving towards us until they had formed a semi-circle around us, while staring unashamedly and whispering. Disconcerted, we hurriedly finished our beer and decided to rid ourselves of the audience by exploring the local market. We set off over the long catwalk between rows of potted palms, to find the onlookers in tow – a steady trickle, close on our heels.

Before long the trickle grew into a stream which gathered force until it reached the proportion of a full-blown procession. When we stopped, the procession stopped. David, who had recommended the hotel, bearded and with the physique of an international rugby player, had obviously not aroused the same interest as three fair-haired, fair-skinned females. It was impossible to browse, bargain or explore. We succeeded in purchasing a bag of small sponge cakes then doubled back, our crocodile in pursuit and chanting 'Hallo' 'Americano' until we reached the relative safety of the hotel.

The reception area remained unmanned. We attempted to find out, from a passing member of staff who spoke a little English, if the requested arrangements had been made for us to be taken by boat to Sipadan. All he could promise was that someone would contact Borneo Divers on the following day. Next we asked if it was possible to hire a boat to take us to the island. It was too far. Finally, while waiting for the contact with Sipadan to be made, we settled for a trip to a nearby deserted island with a local boatman on the following day.

Signalled by a wailing muezzin, darkness fell in tropical style swallowing the coastline. Across the sea massive cumulus clouds, lit by explosions of red light and spasmodically split by lightning, assembled over distant Philippine islands. Pellets of rain bounced from the sea and ricocheted from the floorboards. Under cover, the restaurant was transformed by neon light, a live band and a Chinese female singer. Then under a row of black umbrellas a procession of glittering coiffured females, accompanied by neatly attired escorts appeared from the surrounding jungle; this captivating scene drew the attention of a further gathering of onlookers and provided an opportunity for us to merge into the background. We ordered a meal of giant prawns, steamed vegetables and rice and more cold beer and then disappeared into our rooms.

As tiredness overcame frustration I was lulled to sleep by the hum of the air-conditioner and the slapping of brown water under the floorboards, oblivious of the traumas being suffered by my daughters. Morning revealed they had experienced a series of unexpected visitors. The first a huge antennae-waving cockroach that eventually shot into one of the cracks in the woodwork. After that scurryings, scrapings and scrabblings kept them from more than fitful dozing. Finally, they switched on the light to see two massive rats swaying from a beam on the ceiling, directly over their heads. Like overweight amateur trapeze artists they wobbled towards a wardrobe and attempted to hide from the light by squeezing behind it. They were too fat. Heads and shoulders disappeared but their bulging backsides and rope tails were left dangling. Meanwhile a procession of huge red ants was in progress across the dressing table carrying remaining pieces of sponge cake aloft like prized trophies.

Morning, too, was full of surprises. The restaurant was closed until lunchtime. No breakfast, no packed lunch, no tea, no coffee and no water. The girl at reception said that if we wanted refreshment we would have to go to the market. After last evening's experience we were loathe to make another trip. Eventually, a local boy was sent to buy us fruit, bread and canned drinks. Next we discovered that there was no snorkel equipment for hire or on sale in Semporna. For a hotel that advertised itself as SEMPORNA TOURISM CENTRE there were a disconcerting number of anomalies. Nevertheless, we consoled ourselves with the promise of a relaxing day of lazing and swimming on and from an idyllic island.

By the time the boy returned with our food and drinks a traditional local bumboat complete with diesel engine was waiting. Abdul, the boat owner – wearing a hat resembling a trilby and dressed in a loose shirt and rolled up jeans – was barefooted and with a cigarette held permanently between his lips. Occupying the only shade, under a makeshift awning, his wife was cutting and cleaning fish and occasionally baling a bucket of sea water to sluice the deck. Nevertheless, the boat was impregnated with the pungent smell of fish. As we ploughed towards the open sea, heading in the direction of the Philippine Islands, the water became emerald and the sky intensely blue. Without shade we resorted to wrapping towels round our heads and shoulders to shield us from the increasingly merciless sun. One and a half hours later a tiny island – a head of jungle circled by a fringe of sand – appeared on the horizon. Abdul skilfully navigated between antlers of coral, visible through the translucent water, and took us onto the fringe of a curved white beach.

Wading through the talcum sand of the deserted island was truly magical. We made for the shade of a nearby palm tree; leaving our sarongs and belongings beneath the tree, we were soon sliding and dipping between the waves and collecting giant-sized conch shells that littered the beach. It was while we were idling in the shallow water, letting the incoming waves lift and deposit us onto the sand, that we noticed some boats anchored off the far side of the island. We assumed they were fishing boats until we heard the incongruous sound of pop music drifting towards us. Then, minutes later, from a crown of palm trees towards the centre of the island a group of dark-skinned males appeared. Barefooted and bare chested, they were dressed in shorts and heading towards us – one of them was cradling an armful of coconuts. By the time we had retreated to the shade of our spindly palm tree and were hurriedly tying sarongs over our swimsuits they had arrived and formed a circle round us.

The coconuts were placed in a row at our feet. One of the men took a gleaming parang from his belt and lopped off the heads as easily as if they were hard-boiled eggs. Next he gestured to us to drink the milk. Taking up crouching positions the men were edging closer, hemming us in. Each man was squatting, staring and smiling and edging forward. Silent, anxious questions juggled between us as we nervously sipped the cool milk. Where were they from? What were their intentions? How could we get away or ask them to move away? We didn't like to refuse to drink the milk in case we offended them but what signal were we giving by accepting?

Our various attempts at language communication failed miserably. The only word we seemed to have in common was 'Hallo'. Just as I was beginning to feel that we were in real danger with no way out of our situation or the tight circle round us I noticed Abdul hovering a few meters away. First he started gesturing to the men, then shouting with the result that they backed off a few meters before resuming their squatting positions but now in a huddle. Then Abdul beckoned to us to leave. Our next move was to snatch up our belongings and head towards the beach where the boat was moored. The men followed, Abdul in their trail. They resumed their squatting positions but now at a distance of some twenty-five feet. Abdul positioned himself between the two camps. He remained smoking and watchful until finally the group set off down the beach. The last we saw of them were their silhouettes against shimmering sky as they paddled a raft towards one of the anchored boats.

On the one hand we were on the idyllic deserted island of dreams – paradise on earth. But earthly versions of paradise have their shortcomings. As morning progressed the overhead sun drained colour from the sky and the demented shrieking of cicadas reached a feverish pitch. Making sure that Abdul and his boat remained in sight, we retreated to the shade of the central clump of palms for our picnic of bananas and sweet bread washed down with warm coke. I had just settled against the curved trunk of a fallen palm tree to read when I heard twigs cracking. Wild pig, I thought or monitor lizard. If it were a pig we would need to climb a tree – if a lizard I would need my camera. Then, moving like shadows through the trees, I saw a group of women and children coming towards us.

Short in stature with dark full-length shawls draped across their heads and shoulders each was carrying a long bladed parang. They made straight for Catriona and Justine, who were sitting under a tree a few meters from me; jabbering and pointing at their skin and, no doubt, blue eyes, their heightened voices echoed a state of high excitement. One woman was so excited she was gesticulating haphazardly with her parang. She probably used it to cut her way through undergrowth or to collect fruit but she looked formidable and my imagination was taking over, stirring uncomfortable thoughts of the white slave trade and piracy. When, after several minutes the jabbering, the intense scrutiny nor the gesticulating lessened. 'Let's go!' I called scrambling to my feet.

Once more we gathered our belongings and retreated towards Abdul and the safety of his boat. The party stood in silence and watched us go then turned and walked back through the trees. We assumed that they were related to the male visitors of that morning and in all probability were from the nearby Philippine Islands.

We arrived at the Floating Hotel to discover that our attempts to make contact with Borneo Divers had failed. We were beginning to believe it was deliberate. It was increasingly obvious that visitors were rare and they could make more money by keeping us in Semporna and arranging trips with local fishermen. This was confirmed when the receptionist assured us that she would find a boatman who would provide us with masks and snorkels and take us to a safe island on the following day. Since, once again, the alternative was to waste the day in Semporna, still hopeful that a boat from Sipadan would eventually turn up we agreed.

On this occasion there were two boat men. If they were as diligent and caring as Abdul had been we decided we should be safe enough and this time we would be able to snorkel and see some of the excellent coral and fish that we had caught glimpses of through the translucent water. The men spoke no English but seemed to understand our requests for masks and snorkels. The elder of the two – referred to as 'boss' by Azhar, his assistant – a short sturdy man, was soon in control.

The day was bright and promising. About an hour after the boat chugged away from the hotel, Azhar circled his eyes with his fingers and pointed to a *kelong* – off-shore wooden fishing platform – across the shimmering water. Masks, we thought and nodded our approval. The boss launched himself in a tiny skiff, leaving us to bob up and down in the relentless sun for a good hour before he returned and proudly presented us each with a pair of goggles. They were the size and shape of swimming goggles but appeared to have been carved from coconut shells. There were no snorkels. We exchanged glances and muttered our disbelief. Then the boss handed me a six foot rusty harpoon.

'You,' he instructed. 'You. You dive!' Unsure if the harpoon was for protection against sharks, or to spear fish for lunch, I attempted to appear grateful.

An hour or so later we were approaching a clump of trees, their roots in water. There was no sign of a beach and we were well out of sight of land or other islands. About fifty metres away from the trees Azhar dropped anchor and the boss gestured to us to swim. The deck of the boat was several metres from the water and we could see chalky rocks below. It was too risky to dive or jump and where was the coral? Eventually, Justine and I, adorned in our coconut-shell goggles, clambered over the side and dropped into the murky water. Catriona had decided to stay on board and watch the proceedings from the safety of the deck.

As soon as we submerged the goggles filled with salt water. It was too deep to stand, there was no beach to swim to and even if there was coral we would be unable to see anything. After a time swimming backwards and forwards alongside the boat, goggles dangling round our necks, became a pointless and tiring activity; only then did we wonder how we were going to get back on board? Finally, with Catriona's intervention the boss let down a tyre on a piece of frayed rope. Somehow, with much ungainly clambering, struggling, pulling and pushing we were both floundering on deck exhausted but utterly relieved to be on board and together.

Once we had recovered, with the help of sign language and gesticulation, we explained that we wanted to go to an island with a beach and where there was coral.

'Like Sipadan,' I suggested hopefully.

Neither man appeared to understand. The boss lit a cigarette and was non-committal. Azhar shrugged his shoulders. Then suddenly, in broken but proficient English, the boss demanded I pay him 1,000 Malaysian Ringgit. Shock from the realisation that he not only understood but spoke reasonable English was heightened by the sudden awareness of the grave danger we faced.

We had been warned to keep our passports, money and tickets with us at all times. They were tucked in the inner pocket of my bag on the deck. In a concerted effort to remain calm I explained that all our money was at the hotel and that the manager would be paying him for the trip on our return. He still insisted that I paid him now and he was asking for five times the agreed figure. Once again, I insisted that the hotel manager would pay him. We had no money with us. He remained unchanged. Now anger took over and I demanded that he take us back to the hotel immediately. This time there was a reaction. Throttle open and belching blue fumes the boat shot into action roaring through the waves.

Surrounded by ocean we had no idea where we were heading. We were helpless and full of unspoken fears. Some one and half hours later when I saw the outline of the mosque and then the hotel relief flooded through me. Then, as we drew near, instead of slowing we roared straight past heading for the water village. Fear and the horrible uncertainty of their intentions returned. Just as I had resigned myself to the worst the boat turned and circled back towards the hotel. Either, the boss had wanted to give us a fright, had a change of mind or he needed to detour because of the tide. Whatever the reason, we were grateful for our lives. After reporting what had happened we left the hotel staff to sort out the boatman and decided to leave Semporna at the earliest opportunity.

While we packed, a boy was sent to the travel agent in the town to change our tickets for a flight to Kota Kinabalu for that evening. This done we were just about to board the hotel mini-bus when something made me check the tickets. One was missing. Whether this was the result of genuine error or of some ulterior motive, the thought of being stranded in humid heat at Tawau's grubby airport was nightmarish. Then a final and ironic touch was provided by the untimely arrival of a boat from Sipadan.

'Hi!' said the friendly American striding towards us with an outstretched hand.

'I'm Randy. I work for Borneo Divers. We heard you were here.'

It was too late. We had had enough of the vicissitudes of the Sulu Sea. Waving him goodbye we returned to reception. Just minutes later we were relieved to be greeted by a staff member waving the missing ticket.

Meanwhile the driver, detailed to take us to the airport, had picked up five of his friends. 'Come for ride,' he explained grinning. We settled in the back row of the mini-bus guarding our luggage, tickets and selves. The youths squeezed together in the seats in front of us. As soon as we were underway they rose, turned and knelt facing us, fixing their eyes on us as if watching a riveting movie on a screen. The radio blared, 'I don't wanna leave him now' and similar assorted sob songs. They continued to stare as we bounced up and down over the pot-holed road. The driver, intent upon demonstrating his race-track skills, hogged the middle of the road swerving violently to miss oncoming traffic. The advantage of the speed in reducing the length of the journey outweighed fears of ending upside down in the bush with our captive audience.

Finally, we were deposited on the doorstep of our hotel in Kota Kinabalu. Recovery was aided by sipping afternoon tea in a room cooled by whirling fans and scented by flowers. As grateful as I was for the safety of our return my mind was still throbbing with memories of the dangers we had been unprepared for and subjected to – of how easy it would have been for the second boatman to take off with our bags and to have left us stranded in the Sulu Sea, especially if Catriona had joined us in the water. I said a silent prayer of thanks for our survival.

The following day when we arrived at my apartment in Singapore it was to be lurched into another world. Among the letters on my doormat was an invitation from The British Council requesting the pleasure of my company at 'a reception for William Golding in the Writer's Bar, Raffles Hotel'. Then a week later a step back in time:

a travel feature on Sandakan – an east coast region of Sabah that is more developed for travellers than Semporna – made the life threatening dangers that we had faced unnervingly real. In the final paragraph Lim Joo-Jock summarised the beauty as well as the dangers:

The Borneo Sea is beautiful and clear, the hidden coves with white beaches inviting, and the reefs brilliant with coral and iridescent fishes but the locals warn against venturing to such little gems for fear of ferocious sea pirates who sneak across the international sea boundary just a few kilometres away.

The Sunday Times, Singapore, September 10th 1988

The following year the untouched beauty of Sipadan Island was confirmed by Jacques Cousteau; when he visited to make his film, *'The Ghost of the Sea Turtle'* (1989), he described the island as 'an untouched piece of art.' His response to the island gave it priority on the world stage.

By the turn of the century things had changed dramatically: the number of visitors had increased and once again the threats that we had faced became horrifying reality: media reports focused on the southern Philippine Islands which had become the stronghold of the Abu Sayyaf Guerrilla Sea Pirates: one of 27 terrorist groups said to have been funded by Osama Bin Laden, responsible for hostage taking and murder. This was to include the taking of 21 hostages from Sipadan Island in 2000 and the abduction of an American couple and 20 others from a resort on Palawan Island in May 2003..

2009: Such was the continuing appeal of Sipadan that in spite of worldwide media reports highlighting the dangers, the number of visitors attracted to its shores was so great that the island and its reefs were under threat. In an attempt to preserve the island and its surrounding waters, it was gazetted as a Marine Protected area. Although resorts were no longer allowed on Sipadan Island, nearby Mabul Island had an increasing number while a resort, standing on shallow sandbanks offshore: Sipadan – Kapalai Dive Resort, Semporna – helped to accommodate the influx of visitors. The twin issues of recreational diving and marine conservation combine and continue to bring this island to the attention of the modern world. Sadly, the pristine island of our dreams so admired by Jacques Cousteau no longer exists.

Rose of the North

A brief encounter with Chiang Mai – Thailand's *Rose of the North* – cannot do it justice. Nevertheless, when my daughter, Justine and I set out with just three days at our disposal, on day one we took a hair-raising ride by tuk-tuk to the Whole Earth Thai Vegetarian Restaurant and acquired some debatable bargains at the night-market famed for inexpensive tribal clothing, handicrafts and antiques – real as well as fake. The highlight of day two was a visit to the magnificent Doi Suthep Temple. On our final day a trip to the Golden Triangle – as famous for its position overlooking three countries as it is infamous for connections with the opium trade – preceded a journey through forested hill country to Mae Sai on the Burmese Border.

Although Chiang Mai is not without the noise and pollution of modern traffic it has an international feel, is far more relaxed and has a friendlier atmosphere than the congested and highly polluted capital, Bangkok. A striking backdrop is provided by the Doi Suthep Mount which rises 1,676 metres above and behind the city, while its 300 temples and the Burmese and Chinese influence on its architecture contribute to its visually striking appearance. Northern Thailand, where the first Thai kingdoms arose, dotted with the ruins of great temples, is home to a number of immigrant hill-tribes. Even though the rights of all people to follow their religious beliefs in Thailand is upheld, the influence of Buddhism on the lives of local people is noticeably strong, so much so that the majority of Thai men are said to become monks at some stage in their lives albeit, sometimes, for as little as a week. The Doi Suthep Temple – a centre for Buddhism – as outstanding for its size and position as it is for its history – had priority status on our visit.

Just sixteen kilometres northwest of the city, a taxi took us on a hairpin switchback ride, climbing twelve km uphill before delivering us to the foot of the mount. Resisting the temptation to take the available cable car to reach the temple we opted for a more spiritually fitting approach by ascending the 300 steps of the dragon staircase. Once we had regained our breath and admired the views over the surrounding countryside we were able to turn our attention to the golden temple. Everything, from the tip-tilted tiered eaves of the rooftops to statues of Buddhas, to the intricately designed chedi, topped by a five tiered umbrella – denoting a heavenly position – gleamed with gold. In his fascinating novel *The Glass Palace,* Amitrav Ghosh draws attention to the significance of the number of tiers to denote status or rank. Thus, when the last king of Burma sees the bullock cart, sent by the British to take him into exile from his palace in Mandalay, he sadly noted that the canopy had seven tiers, the number allotted to noblemen, not nine the number due to a king.

With its tip-tilted and tiered eaves Wat Phrathat Doi Suthep, first established under King Keu Na in AD 1383, is reminiscent of both Burmese and Chinese architecture. The overwhelming golden theme continues in a cloister where a line of Buddhas, dressed in golden flowing robes are seated on golden thrones. We were making donations to purchase pieces of gold leaf to attach as prayer offerings to another seated Buddha when we were distracted by the resonant tones of twelve-foot high brass bell. We had already admired the bell, noted and even tentatively touched the tongue hanging below its rim reaching just above ground level. Nearby, a large placard reading 'Please Do Not Shake The Bell' was evidence of the temptation others had succumbed to.

Now, its tolling summoned the monks to lunch and we hurried to watch the procession. Dressed in their traditional saffron robes and carrying food containers, resembling lanterns in shape, they filed past followed by a boy monk of no more than ten years; with a closely shaven head and dressed like his elders he joined the procession. Symbols of both the past and the present, they carried with them an enviable sense of calm dignity and peace acquired by those who place spiritual values above material concerns.

*****

Trekking to visit the hill-tribes of northern Thailand is a main tourist attraction in this region and can be arranged to suit individual needs. In the limited time available to us we hoped to visit one of the more remote tribal villages en route to Thailand's Golden Triangle: the meeting place of Burma, Laos and Thailand and finally reach the Burmese border. By hiring a guide and a car we estimated that we could accomplish this in one day.

The northern tribes, living in the remote scattered settlements in the forested hills north of Chiang Mai, have their origins in China and Tibet and bring with them their own customs and religions. Poverty and isolation from mainstream Thailand is what the tribes have in common. In the past, with those tribes living at 1,000 meters or more, where the opium poppy flourishes, opium growing was the main cash crop and offered an escape from poverty. No longer acceptable by law, government schemes to introduce alternative cash crops have been inaugurated.

In the capable hands of a driver and our Thai guide, named Ping – like the river straddled by Chiang Mai – we headed north-west towards Chiang Rai – the gateway to the Golden Triangle. We had been travelling for an hour or so when Ping asked the driver to stop at the roadside where some roughly made stalls were manned by local people selling hand-made crafts. The reason for the location of the stalls soon became clear. Ping directed us to a hole in the ground where water from a hot spring bubbled above boiling point. Suddenly we were surrounded by a group of children vying with each other to sell us bantam eggs. We settled the dispute by dividing our purchases between the two rival groups. Meanwhile the eggs were placed in a small fishing net and we were invited to squat by the mud-hole and suspend the net into the churning water. A few minutes later we lifted them out and added hard-boiled eggs to our packed lunch. Further north we stopped once again – this time to walk across the slatted wooden bridge which spans the Mae Sai River. Beneath us tumbled an impressive waterfall.

As we continued along the road the hilly terrain and forested land increased and sadly, so did the number of forest fires. The air was heavy with smoke. Then the driver took a detour off the main route and followed a red dusty track to a hill-tribe settlement of Lawa people – thought to have been among the first to have migrated to the hills of northern Thailand. It was like stepping back in time. A buffalo wandered onto the track and stopped in front of our vehicle to scratch itself while a buffalo-drawn cart with a man sitting astride newly cut poles approached us from the village. Then an elephant carrying four villagers strolled nonchalantly towards us. In the village centre several men were engaged in attaching layers of ready prepared strips of dried palm-fronds to thatch the roof of a house.

Remarkably, on our return journey, we saw that the roof had been completed. The spacious wooden village houses were all on stilts and had wide overhanging thatched rooftops reaching almost to the ground in the recognised style of the Lawa people. Unlike reports of the tourist-wise behaviour of inhabitants in the more accessible tribal villages further south – apart from a handful of small children eager to show and sell us hand-made beaded bracelets and necklaces –

these villagers waved to us, got on with their activities and appeared happy for us to wander through their settlement with the children taking on the role of escorts.

Back on the main route we were nearing the outskirts of Chiang Saen. Once a walled fortified city sprawling along the banks of the Mekong River, the ancient settlement dates back to the 13th century; seized by the Burmese in 1558 and held by them until 1804 when King Rama I of Siam recaptured the city and burned it to the ground. The premise: we had to destroy it to save it. Abandoned for seventy years it was finally rebuilt by Chao Inta, a son of the Prince of Lumpoon.

It was in the atmospheric setting of its ancient ruins, set amongst sheltering trees that we decided to have our picnic. Ping directed the driver to a spot near a *stupa* – conical shaped monument used to inter Buddhist relics – marking the ramparts of the ancient site: the great stone walls reminded me of Sri Lanka's huge dagobas and ancient Buddhist settlements. It was also a reminder of the Thai absorption of the basic tenets of Theravada Buddhism, inherited from Sri Lanka; a belief that all life is suffering and that man can only be freed from the eternal cycle of rebirth through prayer and meditation. In this thought-provoking atmosphere, under the shade of whispering trees, we tucked into our sandwiches and still warm hard-boiled eggs.

When we finally arrived at the Golden Triangle we climbed to the top of a small hill with extensive views across the huge meandering loops of the Mekong River and its tributary which separate Burma, Thailand and Laos: a physical and symbolic meeting and dividing place of countries and cultures; it was both scenically beautiful and strangely moving. As we descended, first one and then a second horse-drawn cart piled high with poppy heads clattered by. Although the growing of poppies for opium was now prohibited it was evident that some of the hill farmers were still involved. Ping explained that most of the farmers have changed and now grow tobacco, tomatoes and other vegetables. At the foot of the hill a string of small roadside cafes and stalls selling local craftwork stretched along the bank of the river.

We had one more visit before we began the long ride back to Chiang Mai. Born in Maymyo, a British hill-station in Burma, I had a burning ambition to set foot on Burmese soil. To satisfy my request Ping directed the driver to the border town of Mae Sai; at that time it was the only official open land crossing between Thailand and Burma. A road market selling lacquered furniture, gems, jade and other goods brought across from Laos and Burma was the first sign that we were approaching the border. Among the lacquer ware I was intrigued to see small octagonal collapsible tables – identical to those my parents brought back with them from Burma many years ago – complete with images of graceful dancing and seated figures in pagoda like settings. Just beyond the market an armed soldier was standing guard at the start of the bridge that spans the Mae Sai River and marks the boundary between the two countries.

Ping explained that only Burmese and Thai nationals are allowed to cross the bridge so it was with some trepidation that I approached the guard, showed him my passport with Maymyo clearly marked as my place of birth, and asked permission to cross onto Burmese soil. The guard nodded his head in approval. Watched by Justine and the bemused Ping I made my short but meaningful crossing to the land where my infant life began, stirring memories of my parents' tales of earth tremors; orchids growing from trees; thieving monkeys causing havoc and playing with beaded curtains; *punka wallahs, dhobi wallahs, ayahs* – remnants of the inherited baggage of a colonial past – a fitting and meaningful end to our travels through the fascinating Land of the Thais.

*****

At the time of my visit (1989) education was not accessible to many of the more remote tribal villages, in Thailand, especially those that could be reached only by foot.

In January 2002 I read the following encouraging report in *Gulf News,* Dubai:

Thailand's Non-Formal Education Department is using elephants to transport teachers along with books and other educational materials to underprivileged tribes, such as the minority Karen, many of whom have never seen a textbook. Training for adults in agricultural techniques and healthcare is also offered. Each team of teachers plans to stop at a village for two days using text books, TV, videotapes and community activities to stimulate interest in learning then they cycle to other villages, returning to each every two or three weeks. Many of the teachers are young graduates, fired by a zeal to help the underprivileged in the hills of Chiang Mai Province.

Gulf News, Dubai, January 2002 [U-Jae, Thailand (AP)]

2008: the Reuters' correspondent report was a poignant reminder of the continuing political unrest in Burma, now Myanmar and of Maymyo, the place of my birth:

Northern Thailand: Reuters Writer/Ed Cropley Maymyo: March 10th 2008

Burma's Last Royal Laments Crumbling Nation. Taw Paya, the sole surviving grandson of Burma's last king, outside his house in Maymyo speaks out against the ruling military regime. 'They have transformed Burma from the rice bowl of Asia into a deeply impoverished international pariah, leading to galloping inflation, deepening poverty and monk-led protests.'

*****

The visit to Thailand was my last journey into Asia from my Singapore base. Before making a final exit, a visit to expatriate friends, previously living and working in Singapore – who had recently set up home in Australia – is captured in the poem *Shifting Horizons*.

Shifting Horizons

Boxing Day. I arrive on your heels.
Gift wrapped. Room 511, striped white
and buttercup yellow, is a stepping-stone.
For a week we live on strawberries
and champagne, pace between encroaching walls
wound tight as caged jaguars. Roots trailing.

Sometimes, I slip into ivory silk
and sit on the balcony, pressed
to the shade of a spindly potted palm.
Between concrete blocks, the sea rolls out and in.
Once we moved as waves. In this strange place
familiar selves fade, new angles glint.

New Year's Eve. From a verandah
we watch fireworks explode over Sydney Harbour.
A slow-motion film: magnificent flowers
unfolding, falling on the falling year.
In a candle lit room, strangers, decked in balloons,
gyrate to scratched rock'n roll.

The *nouveau riche* thrive like mushrooms
in suburbia. *Les uns, les autres.*
Later, we dance and almost find each other.
A new decade: stretched on the beach,
a desert between us. Hot winds strips my skin
like gum trees' bark. At Alice Springs
the night's as bright as a crystal chandelier.
We could diet in the desert. Catch desert rats.
Get drunk on space.

We take the road to the hills, blue
with feathery eucalyptus: opium of gods
and dozing koalas, pull in beneath
the twisted limbs of a ghost gum. Endless trees,
insistent shrilling cicadas, shimmering air
brittle as glass blown by this fierce sun.

The horizon tilts. The road burns
and thrums through rushing leaves,
dips over skeletal creeks – pebble-dashed,
root-bound – slows through the neat rows
of baked suburbia to Room 511.

I prefer to imagine you at your Belgium farmhouse,
logging in the woods, dogs soporific
by the fireplace, than in these tidy streets.
I'll write from Togo or Brazil,
or maybe from the shade of *les pins parapluies*

in the south of France. I'll become fluent in French.
You'll learn Japanese with a French accent.
We'll perfect communication.

A last spin over the cart-wheeling bridge,
the shelled opera house shining
like Aphrodite newly risen.
From the air, raging bushfires diminish
to smouldering garden heaps; distance stretches
like gold, finely spun.

The trapped house suffocates.
I wander from room to room between
sleeping Buddhas, throw open windows
and doors, exchange heat for heat.
The wilting garden, buried in scented leaves,
sinks in darkness and the cicadas' tragic chorus.

Soon, the family will return,
olive skinned from their Christmas Island.
Lit with smiles. Open-armed.
Face to face with a humming fan
I drift towards sleep. Rehearse departures.
At first light the kookaburra's maniacal cry
will waken me and tell the people of the sky
to release the sun.

*****

As I packed and made preparations to leave Singapore I searched the atlas for a convenient and interesting stopover on the long haul home. I had romantic notions about Istanbul – not so much Istanbul as Constantinople and its evocative past. From the air, first impressions of this vast metropolis stretching across two waterways – the Golden Horn and the Bosphorus and straddling Europe and Asia – were of the contrast between the splendour and beauty of skyward reaching domes and spiralling minarets and the sheer ugliness of miles of sprawling concrete.

Down and Out in Istanbul

A small hotel, in the old city, within easy walking distance of major historical sites: these were the priorities for a short stay in Istanbul. It was June and the tourist season was in full swing as were the poor who swarm in from the countryside during the summer months to make as much money as possible to keep them alive during the winter. They lined the narrow streets selling leather belts, socks, perfume and spinning-tops – expertly demonstrating the performance of the latter on the backs of their hands, knees or street with equal ease.

Young boys vied with each other to clean the shoes of passers by. Older men, propping up doorways to shops, tried to lure window-shoppers inside to buy gold, leather goods or carpets. Failure to sell led to propositions, some less veiled than others. Every few steps I was the target of a male who wanted to sell me something, quickly followed by efforts to entice me into a shop, buy me a drink, clean my shoes or lure me up an alley. To keep the rogues and hassling at bay I learnt that the best policy was to keep walking and look straight ahead; any response, no matter how negative or aggressive was construed as an invitation to further pursuit and means of persuasion. Once again, on my travels, I was on foot, alone and vulnerable but firmly intent on my priority of reaching Saint Sophia Cathedral: *Hagia Sophia, Sancta Sophia.*

My visit was quite literally a flying one, not allowing sufficient time to explore the museum that the cathedral, then mosque it became in 1935, when taken over by Turkey. When I finally arrived, just standing before the great heavenward thrusting dome was enough to roll back the years to the Byzantine era and to the day of its birth in AD 537. Its complex history started when the emperor Constantine I decided to move the seat of the empire from Rome to Byzantium in the early 4th century. The emperor's dream of a great church in Constantinople – the new heart of Christianity – was finally realised by his son Constantine II. Although this church and its successor were both destroyed by rioting mobs it was the Emperor Justinian's vision of a larger, grander church that succeeded its predecessors and exists to this very day. The Basilica of the Patriarch of Constantinople and the religious focal point of the Eastern Orthodox Church for nearly 1,000 years, it remains a powerful tribute to Justinian and to early Christianity. And then in 1453 the Ottomans came, desecrated and took over *Hagia Sophia*, finally using it as a model not only for the Blue Mosque in Istanbul but for Ottoman mosques throughout the Muslim world.

In spite of the four spiked minarets standing guard and claiming possession of the coveted cathedral, the purity of form of the great Christian dome remained as awe-inspiring on this day as it had been to the emperor. When Justinian arrived to dedicate his breath-taking church of *Hagia Sophia* – Holy Wisdom – he is said to have cried out: *'Solomon, I have surpassed thee'*. To endorse this, the emperor then turned his attention to building a basilica in Jerusalem: the *Nea* (New) Church of Saint Mary, Mother of God – designed to over-shadow Solomon's Temple.

My fascination with the incredible achievements of the Emperor Justinian went beyond his spreading of the universal Christian Empire throughout the Mediterranean and across North Africa to a legend of an extraordinary encounter he had in Syria – an encounter which resulted in the building of the shrine of *Notre Dame de*

Seidnaya – Our Lady of *Seidnaya*. While on a hunting expedition, the emperor is said to have chased a stag onto a rocky outcrop. Just as he was about to draw his bow, the stag changed into the Virgin Mary who commanded Justinian to build a convent on the site. The explanation of the legend's etymological origin – Aramaic *Seidnaya* means both 'our lady' and 'hunting place' – is what gives substance to this story.

Furthermore, it is in the chapel, attached to the convent of Our Lady of Seidnaya – built at that very place – that an icon of the Virgin, attributed to Saint Luke, is venerated to this day by both Christians and Muslims. The belief that this remarkable icon sheds tears was attested to by the eminent travel writer Colin Thubron; when he visited the convent in 1996, he claimed to have witnessed a miracle when standing before the icon of *Notre Dame de Seidnaya*, the face streamed with tears.

Speedy mind-set adjustments – from monasteries and miracles to strategies for escape from pursuing road-side vendors – took place on the route back to the hotel. Reality set in when I arrived: my requested room with a view did have a view – over a building site. Added to this the noise of drilling and hammering was now in competition with the roar of traffic below, while billowing dust mingled with yellow clouds of pollution already suffocating the city was closing in on the hotel.

After a restless night I arrived for breakfast to discover that I was sharing the hotel with a handful of Americans and a group-tour of retired French couples. While the French were bent on enjoying themselves, the Americans' voices were raised in complaint about overdone, instant or 'muddy' Turkish coffee. Meanwhile, I was enjoying orange juice and toast; the decor of the duck-egg blue dining room; perfume from the vases of sweet williams and carnations, decorating each table and the bird's-eye view I had of waiters practising their waiting skills. One, carrying a breakfast tray, spilt coffee over the sugar knobs before he reached the lift and had to go back and start again, while another balancing a stack of baskets of bread rolls on one upturned hand, dropped the lot and thinking he hadn't been seen, picked them up and carried on in the style of *Down and Out in Istanbul.*

It was while I was waiting for transport to go on a boat trip to Buyukada Island, in the Marmara Sea, that I was inundated by the French party. For one moment I thought I was to share the trip with them then, to my relief, they disappeared into a waiting coach at a sprightly pace. Shortly after, Yilmaz, my university-student guide, arrived. Like many other students, in dire need of money, she had presented her programme of study to the tour operator at the hotel, who slotted her free time into the busy summer schedule.

Yilmaz organised a taxi and escorted me on board a boat at the quay; as she did so she explained that *Buyukada* (Big Island) was the largest of six main islands, known as Princes' Islands. From my research I understood that it was the Byzantine Emperor Justin II who had a palace and monastery built on Buyukada in AD 569 and that he was the prince who gave the islands their name. More monasteries followed; in the ensuing centuries they became prisons for emperors, empresses and patriarchs who fell out of favour on the mainland. It was when the Ottomans took over that the islands became summer resorts for Istanbul's wealthy families. Today, the larger islands are favoured places to take visitors. Yilmaz explained that of the smaller islands, one is known for its hospital where asthmatic patients are sent to recover from the polluted air of the city; another for swimming only – is used largely by young couples at weekends and for school picnics during the week, while the last houses a security prison.

As we set sail we had superb views of ancient mosques and their skyward reaching minarets gracing the skyline. Then a group of hawkers, with armfuls of *Lacoste* sweaters, magically appeared at the same time as a biting wind from the sea. It was the first time I remember being pleased to see a hawker since arriving in the East, fresh to the novelty of bargaining. This one was in luck. I bought the largest sweater I could find. It was warm and looked as genuine as the real thing. By the time we arrived the island was bathed in sunlight. The walkway from the jetty led past wooden colonial-style houses, shutters closed; balconies overlooked sleepy, tree-lined streets leading to the central square where pony-driven carts – the only transport on the island – waited for passengers from the ferry.

A major highlight of the island is the still serving Monastery of Saint George; built under the patronage of Justin II in AD 569, it is a place where – like the Convent of Seidnaya, in Syria – to this day, both Muslims and Christians come to light candles and pray. A further reminder that it is the mutual tolerance and shared customs of Eastern Christians and Muslims that have enabled them to live and pray side by side for half a millennia. Sadly, a visit to the monastery was not on the agenda of our sightseeing tour of the island.

Since I was alone I joined an Italian couple and their small son, Randolph. Before long the houses stopped and we began a gentle clip-clop uphill. Sudden glimpses of sea between fig trees, lining the route, gradually gave way to forests of pine where ponies wandered free. Between Randolph's bronchial cough and other attention seeking tactics I learnt that the family divided their time between living in an apartment in Hampstead and a villa in Tuscany.

I spent most of my time guarding myself from Randolph's well-distributed germs and protecting my shins from blows from his swinging feet. 'Mama' and 'Papa' responded to Randolph's antics by alternately correcting and pampering him. Then as we were rounding a corner a sudden increase in the clatter and pace of hooves heralded the arrival of another pony and cart. It was close on our heels and before long fully bent on overtaking us. The road was narrow and we were approaching a bend. What had been a leisurely jog uphill was turning into something resembling a chariot race. Just as the contending pony's head reached the neck of our startled beast, it took fright and reared baring its teeth and tipping the cart over to one side.

Dressed in a mini skirt and stiletto heels, Mama gave a high-pitched squeal and with a show of surprising athleticism, leapt over the side. The rest of us, hanging on but still in our seats, stared with disbelief as she fell and rolled inelegantly into the hedgerow. Fortunately, she wasn't injured but she was very angry, especially with Papa who had not leapt to her rescue. She struggled to her feet, patting her bouffant hairdo into place and spitting fire about his lack of gallantry. His calm response was that he had been concerned for the safety of his son.

The down hill trip and boat ride home were fairly leisurely and uneventful, if increasingly cold. By late afternoon I was recovering at the hotel by making my way through a large pot of tea when, once again, I was distracted by the arrival of the French visitors. Their guide announced that they must be ready in half an hour for the coach which was taking them to a restaurant for dinner. Apart from a couple of wayward males, who looked guiltily from side to side before heading straight for the bar, they disappeared into lifts and through doorways.

As I was leaving the restaurant, Mohammed, the hotel receptionist, informed me that he also worked as a part-time guide and offered to take me on a private tour to see Istanbul by night from a hilltop across the bridge spanning Europe and Asia. I have romantic notions about global lines which both separate and join countries and can still remember the feeling of excitement I experienced as a child when I stood astride the Greenwich Meridian. More recent memories were of the spectacular view of Thailand's Golden Triangle when I stood with my feet in Thailand and looked down on the Mekong River with Burma on the left and Laos on the right. This was to be my last night in Istanbul so abandoning caution I accepted his invitation. We arranged to meet in the reception area at eight p.m.

At the agreed time Mohammed escorted me to his ancient Vauxhall. We set off, rumbling through the congested city, our belching fumes contributing to the haze hanging over us, across the celebrated bridge onto what was supposed to be a six lane motor way. The utter chaos of racing traffic and screeching brakes made tackling England's M25 on a Friday evening seem like a quiet drive along a country lane.

We were somewhere in the centre of a river of thunderous vehicles and starting to go uphill when the engine of the Vauxhall growled in a sort of protest, puttered and petered out. It was growing dark and we were now stationary in a hot-bed of surging metal that roared and honked as it attempted to diverge round us in a glare of lights and billowing fumes. 'This is it!' I thought – not the first time on my travels – momentarily closing my eyes. Undeterred, Mohammed started to free-wheel, in reverse, through oncoming vehicles then across swerving, swearing lanes to the roadside. The driver from another abandoned vehicle joined us. They both lit cigarettes and bent their heads over the overheated engine. I got out, walked 20 metres away along the juddering tarmac and hailed a taxi to take me back to the hotel.

At two a.m. I was woken by the phone. Mohammed was calling to say he had just got back with his car and could he take a shower in my room? I put the phone down, leaving it off the receiver, checked that my door was securely locked and resolved that my days of travelling alone were over.

My resolution didn't last long. Just months later I was preparing to set off once more – not only was I alone but returning to the wilds of Borneo. Opportunities for further travels with like-minded expatriate companions was the deciding factor in accepting a position as an English Language Instructor in Brunei. I had yet to learn about the downsides of life in this remote overseas posting.

Between Jungle & Sea

A Canadian cedar house, wedged between jungle and sea, where early morning birdsong was the clatter of horn-bills' beaks. This was my home in Kuala Belait, on Brunei's border with Sarawak. It didn't take long to discover that it was a wild and dangerous ex-pat posting. In addition to the wilderness surrounds, the recent tightening of strict Islamic law added considerable tension. Just prior to my arrival the last practising Catholic priest had been deported. At Christmas he made a secret return to say mass in an expatriate neighbour's garage. I attended and spent the entire service expecting to hear and feel gun shots in my back. Just a week previously violent destruction – by armed police – of a statue of Father Christmas and his sleigh, on display outside the local expatriate food-store, had fired my imagination. Perhaps the most frightening experience was arrest for failing to get off the road when the sultan and his entourage were expected on their way to the palace – the same route taken by expatriates travelling from Brunei's capital, Bandar Seri Begawan, to Kuala Belait. Escorted to the main police station I was interrogated for over an hour before being released.

There was no doubt about it – membership of Shell Petroleum Company's Social and Sailing Club was the reward for the downsides to life in Brunei. However, even this was not without its dangers: while the 470 sailors shared the nearby Belait River with sharks, Hobie Cat sailors and divers, off abandoned oil-rigs, shared the greater expanse of the South China Sea with both sharks and a range of equally intimidating predators. An unexpected close encounter is captured in the poem *Hobie Cat Sunday*.

Hobie Cat Sunday

A late start to the blood-red strains
of Bruch's violin concerto: bacon, eggs, proper coffee
– one eye on the casuarinas, willing them to bend –
then to the boat-shed. We heave the Hobie onto a trolley,
lug her to the beach: a handicapped maiden aunt.

Dressed and afloat she's a nubile queen.
Wind in her lungs she sings: deep throated monotone
– plaintive as the attenuated note from a violin –
takes us flying till your trapeze line twangs apart.
You lean on air, cling to the tiller. It snaps

leaving a twig in your hand. Baton aloft you drop
into a hole in the South China Sea, catapult me
through cartwheeling rigging. Trapped below
between taut strings I feel my way to air,
hold bleeding arms like trophies. *'Get on!'* you yell,

torpedoing towards me. *'Shark!'* We flounder
onto the sideways hull, haul the Hobie to her feet.
She tosses her head, streaks for the beach,
sails thrumming. The tip of a silver fin
slices waves – deft as a hot knife through ice-cream.

Blood like red rain in the wind.

Land of Beautiful Harbours

In addition to the excitement of Hobie Cat sailing in the South China Sea there were opportunities to sail to and from off-shore islands in the club's 38' sailing yacht, *The Star of Siam*. Apart from the sailing it was the opportunity to stock up on supplies of alcohol – not available in 'dry' Brunei – that was an added incentive; local people risked jail by selling alcohol to Brunei's expatriate sailors. These exploits were also preparation for an excursion from Brunei to and round Palawan Island, the most remote and isolated of the larger islands of the Philippine Archipelago: a popular venue for sailors from the club, it was an opportunity I could not resist. In March 1991, I joined the captain and fellow intrepid crew members for a two week cruise round *Palawan Island* – Land of Beautiful Harbours – in *The Star of Siam*.

Day 1

In a light wind and light sea, we left Muara Port, sails and expectations flying. Minutes later we passed out of Muara Channel into Brunei Bay, en route for the South China Sea and before long were in sight of our weekend islands of Pulau Kuraman, Rusukan Kecil and neighbouring Rusukan Besar when several fishing boats laden with supplies of beer, wine and spirits homed in on us like bullets. The local fishermen can smell expatriates from 'dry' Brunei on the wind and are willing to risk confiscation of their boats and jail for the quick profits made from trafficking in alcohol. We exchanged dollars and T-shirts for supplies of beer and a box of white wine; crammed as many cans of beer into the ice-box as we could and stacked the rest with the neatly packed piles of tinned and dry food.

Under Bruneian Law no alcohol can be sold in the country. Non-Muslims were allowed to bring two bottles of spirits through customs but this must not be consumed in public and must not be taken out of the country. Before the trip we had decided that anyone with 'special needs' must make his/her own provisions. I am not a beer drinker, unless there is no choice as is often the case in Brunei. I had saved a bottle of gin bought at Duty Free on a trip to Singapore and transferred the contents to an empty plastic bottle of Spa Water. Tim, the captain, had printed on it in large indelible letters: THIS IS NOT WATER! I estimated there should be enough to allow for one or two G & Ts at sundown to last for two weeks. Once we had loaded and packed all the black-market supplies we set off on the estimated four days and four nights sailing until we reached our first planned anchorage in Bacuit Bay.

That evening was our first experience of preparing a hot meal for six on two swaying gas burners. The oven was defunct and the new one, on order, had not arrived. This had infuriated but not surprised us. Nothing arrives on time in Brunei. Telephones break down and are not repaired for months; parcels arrive late and opened or not at all. Letters addressed to Negara Brunei Darussalam, the country's full title, were likely to travel via Dar es Salaam in East Africa and could take months if not years to arrive. Brunei had inherited and retained the nightmare of colonial bureaucracy but was without the infrastructure or motivation to support it. Miraculously, our new and obligatory life raft had arrived. We estimated that we could survive without the oven.

At this stage preparation of the evening meal in the primitive and sauna conditions of the galley was a novelty and a challenge. Madge, who appeared to be the most practical and domesticated member of crew, cheerfully took control. Since she was the only person without sailing experience, she was also eager to prove her worth. We were soon hungrily devouring the contents of tinned vegetable soup with added potatoes. As the sun slipped into the sea and the first stars appeared we sipped cold beer and began to get to know each other. We were going to live closer than a family for two weeks and with less privacy than in a cramped two bedroom flat. It was time for revelations about ourselves and our sailing experiences.

There were three common factors among the crew: we were all expatriates living in or near Kuala Belait; we were members of Shell Boat and Sailing Club and we all knew or were acquainted with Tim. Considering that he was captain of the Hobie fleet, one of the captains of the *Star of Siam* and Rear Commodore of the boat club, this was hardly surprising. This was his third cruise to the Philippines: once as crew, and a year ago as skipper for the first time. Now, as captain at the wheel of the *Star,* he was in his element giving orders to his crew to pull on ropes, hoist or drop sails, estimate and plot positions. Never happier than when surrounded by his family in the cockpit – a captive audience for his yarns – he had an optimistic belief that, whatever the conditions, his crew shared his deep love of the sea and sailing and this love would be sufficient to bind us in friendship during and beyond the duration of the cruise.

David and his Chinese wife Anna, recently married, looked upon the cruise as a second honeymoon. David confessed that really he was a Club Med freak. It was Anna's choice to come on the cruise. Anna's silence was taken as assent. She appeared to be as reticent as David was voluble. They both had some sailing experience – more recently racing 470 dinghies on the crocodile infested River Belait that separates Brunei from neighbouring Sarawak.

Phil, a regular 470 dinghy sailor, was eager to extend his sailing experience. He had become ill on the previous cruise to Palawan and was determined to compensate for all he had missed. Although Madge had never sailed, she was a social member of the sailing club and had been inspired by our enthusiasm; her comment that she hoped we would benefit from her practical housekeeping and cooking skills was favourably received; her final comment that she was looking forward to a rest drew quizzical expressions from the more experienced sailors.

As for me, before arriving in Brunei some eighteen months ago, my sailing experience had been limited to wind-surfing in Singapore and the occasional weekend as a passenger on a yacht from Changi Yacht Club, when my primary duty had been to fill wine glasses. Since arriving in Brunei I had learnt to sail Hobie Cats in the wild South China Sea and had acted as crew on several weekend trips to local islands on the *Star*. I had just missed the last Philippines trip, a year ago, and spent the long months between increasing my competence by gaining a qualification in the Theory of Navigation & Seamanship, earning me the role of first mate. My hesitancy, about how I would cope with being confined for days and nights with little known companions was overridden by my expectations.

Self-revelations over, it was time to wash-up. We decided that the chore would be more comfortable carried out on deck. Two buckets of sea-water were uphauled: one with added detergent for washing, one without for rinsing. Madge in control, the task was soon completed. Novelty and relatively calm sea conditions contributed to the ease of the operation and to the general air of conviviality. Now it was time for the skipper to allocate watches for the night: Phil and Madge were on the early watch from eight p.m. till midnight; David and Anna the dreaded middle-watch from midnight till four a.m., while Tim and I had the luxury of looking forward to eight hours sleep before the more favourable dawn-watch.

It didn't take long to get to know our home-at-sea for the next two weeks. Below deck was compact and open-plan. This included the loo – the door had no lock and frequently refused to stay closed. Even when it did the overhead hatch was invariably open and in favourable weather someone was usually sunbathing or sun hiding alongside it. Somewhat smaller than its counterpart on a large aircraft it required considerable skill to use, especially in rough seas. In fact, on a previous trip I found that remaining upright required the expertise of a world class gymnast. At the foot of the steps, leading from the cockpit, was the galley housing a sink, cooker, ice-box and cupboards lining every inch of wall space.

Night time accommodation was organised in various berths slotted alongside the galley, navigating equipment, between storage cupboards and in the dining area; the more luxurious forward cabin was the prerogative of the skipper; in the role of first mate I was offered a slot in the relatively generous available space. A large overhead hatch provided welcome ventilation. Armed with sleeping bags and pillows everyone's dream was to sleep on deck beneath a canopy of stars.

Shopping for the trip had been based on a list passed down from last year's crew on a similar expedition. There were six people to cater for and limited storage space. The bulk of the provisions had to be tinned or dried. There was also limited space in the ice-box for perishable food which would otherwise perish within twenty-four hours in the humid heat. Drinks were a priority and included boxes of bottled water and thirst quenching varieties of soft drinks to replace all the body fluids we were going to lose. Several trips to the local supermarket catered for most of our needs. We found that we were in competition for bulk with a contingent of Gurkha soldiers – employed by the sultan to guard the Bruneian borders – they were stocking up for a lengthy jungle trek.

Perishable food that rampant mould didn't attack would undoubtedly keep the resident cockroaches happy. They devour anything they can penetrate and tend to eat their way through in a straight line. On a previous weekend trip two loaves, left in a locker, were tunnelled through from end to end, leaving a hole that looked like a miniature model of the Channel Tunnel. They also gorged another tunnel through four packets of cereal that were standing side by side. Risk of disease meant that the remaining contents had to go overboard.

Although the *Star of Siam* was repeatedly sprayed and scoured between trips, and we took precautions by spraying all tins and cartons to kill undetected eggs before bringing them on board, we knew that all we could hope to achieve was a reduction in numbers. We had to learn to share our accommodation with cockroaches just as we had to learn to share the ocean with sharks.

Once we had stored all the dried and tinned food, we tied a string hammock over the dining table and filled it with fresh fruit. After a few hours, below deck was filled with an exotic aroma.

By the time Tim had briefed the crew about compass headings and what to expect and look out for on particular watches we had sailed past Labuan Island into the South China Sea and could see the retreating black outline of Sabah's mountainous west coast. There would be no more land ahead and the next accurate fix we could expect was from a lighted beacon on Jahat Shoals, shortly after midnight. Leaving Phil and Madge at the helm the rest of us descended into sticky aromatic heat, crawled onto and into respective berths and were soon rocked to sleep by the rhythm of the boat.

Day 2

I was woken at two a.m. by someone bending over Tim and shaking him. It was David, concerned that he missed the light on Jahat Shoals. Tim got up. I went back to sleep. Later, I learnt that at about midnight David had sailed through a fishing fleet. Tim decided that the fleet was probably centred on the shallow waters and rich fishing grounds round Jahat Shoals thus, he had been unable to identify the beacon's light among the lights of the boats. Another, just as viable, explanation was that the light was no longer working. In fact we considered it a bonus to find a charted light that did operate in these waters. Fortunately, we weren't totally reliant on lighted beacons but plotted our headings with the help of Satnav (satellite navigation). Nevertheless, it was good to be able to confirm our position with a lighted beacon, especially when we knew we wouldn't see land for days. With the help of Tim and Satnav we were soon on course, with the possible danger of floundering on rocks west of the shoals behind us.

*****

The air was cool; the sky dizzy with stars. Armed with mugs of tea we revived sufficiently to plot our position then, since the wind had dropped, Tim switched on the engine and put the controls in the capable hands of George, the auto-pilot. It was eerie sitting on the bench beside the wheel, watching it slip from side to side with no tangible presence to guide it. We were heading towards the first glimmer of light nudging sky from sea on the eastern horizon. A rosy tinge spread across blotting-paper sky, seeping into pale green which, in turn, merged into duck-egg blue. One by one the nearest stars dissolved and the red lip of sun appeared and grew into a huge orange ball which slipped like liquid over the horizon.

As morning progressed, heat from the sun grew intense, the sea became choppy and the wind was up. Bedraggled members of the crew appeared – except Anna. She wasn't seen for the entire day. Everyone was feeling nauseous. Below deck was insufferably hot, impossible to balance and the aroma was becoming more pungent than exotic. George and the engine were made redundant. By mid-day we were sailing with the taff-rails in the water, waves grew into hills and rolled towards us crashing across the deck. Those on the windward side were under constant attack from lashing spray and remained seated by pressing their feet against the opposite benches. The only place to be was in the cockpit. We took turns to steer and inadvertently develop our biceps.

Now, Tim was at the helm giving instructions. Strapped into harnesses, Phil and David did manly things about the deck; Madge was learning how to sheet in and use the winch and I was the general dogsbody – another privilege of being the skipper's mate.

There were two highlights during the day: a brief glimpse of a distant school of dolphins, and the loss of a bucket during Madge's valiant attempt to wash-up. Fortunately, it was empty. Tim refused to do a man overboard drill to save it. As darkness fell, conditions worsened. Below deck the heat was rampant and the roller-coasting boat was lurching forwards and sideways in gargantuan leaps. Movement on the yacht had to be conducted in short bursts and by aiming for something to hang on before the next spurt. Nobody was interested in cooking or eating. In the end we compromised and boiled water to make a Maggi-Mee noodle concoction. It was hot and required little effort to prepare. Anna still hadn't appeared.

'It was her choice,' David reminded us. 'I wanted to go to Club Med.' He was wearing a Club Med T-shirt to prove it.

Tim and I had been up since four a.m. nevertheless, we had to remain awake and alert until midnight. Things could get worse. They did. The lights failed. Although we were unlikely to encounter anything larger than a fishing vessel, since we couldn't be seen it was up to us to keep clear. Steering by shining a torch on the compass needle was a strain. When it was my turn I aligned the tip of the boom with a transit through the two westward stars of The Plough, checking the compass needle from time to time. After an hour I was feeling star-crazy. We took turns to read and plot Satnav fixes.

I was steadily gathering bruises from falling up and down the galley steps and attempting to balance over the chart table. This was best accomplished by wedging my heels against the wall behind me and placing my elbows firmly on the table leaving my hands free for plotting fixes. Back and legs were positioned at ten to five o'clock. I decided that long legs were a disadvantage. My centre of gravity wasn't low enough. I wished I had short legs. I wished I pumped iron instead of writing poems. I wished I hadn't come. Any thoughts I harboured about a world cruise had been doused long-since.

Midnight finally arrived. Below deck anything that could rattle, bang or slide was doing so. The groaning hammock of fruit that had been strung over the dining table was lurching from side to side. I summoned the energy to battle with the loo, gained several more bruises and prepared myself for the next hurdle: climbing onto the berth. I had just got my knees onto the outer wooden ledge when the boat lurched and rolled. I shot forward like a missile and was thrown against the leeward wall – my head whiplashed after me. I curled in a foetal position moaning and nursing the pain. Then Tim arrived on all fours. We decided that the only way to survive was by lying across the cabin, feet pressed against the leeward wall. It was like trying to sleep standing up and leaning against a wall that lunged between angles of 120 and 160 degrees. Over our heads the closed hatch kept the deluge out and the heat in. Finally, sleep, that had seemed an impossible luxury, fell like an executioner's axe.

Day 3

I surfaced at about ten a.m. to find the sun shining, Anna up and celebrating the return of her appetite by tucking into a bowl of noodles. The sea and wind had subsided so much that the engine and George had been re-employed. While Tim was engaged mending the electrics the rest of us set about righting the havoc above and below deck from the night before. This included removing quantities of bruised and putrid fruit from the hammock. The major culprits appeared to be a fermenting pineapple and some oranges that had been squashed by a watermelon. This done the next task was to spruce ourselves up. Although there was a shower, of sorts, we couldn't afford to be extravagant with our fresh water supplies.

Tim explained the accepted procedure for bath-time on the *Star*. First the pre-requisite buckets of seawater except – as everyone reminded Madge – it was now one bucket. While the crew were stripping down to swimwear, shampooing and lathering, Tim fastened three buoys at intervals along a piece of rope about fifty metres in length. The rope was attached to the stern and dropped into the water. Next he turned the engine off and headed up-wind to slow us down as much as possible. Then while Tim and I remained on board as look-outs, one by one the others jumped or dived into the waves and made for the buoys leaving trails of soapy bubbles. Our duty was to make sure that no-one missed the safety line and was left behind, and we had to be ready to give the alert if a shark appeared.

As divers off abandoned oil rigs and reefs in the South China Sea, we had become accustomed to the idea of sharing the ocean with sharks and have on occasions swum alongside reef and whale sharks.

Like divers, sharks are attracted to the bracings of the rigs which are covered in coral and visited by a wide variety and large numbers of tropical fish. When diving we were with other experienced divers and had the bracings or reef-wall to retreat to for security. Whether, when face to face with an inquisitive shark I would remain calm enough to give it a sharp blow on the snout, fins or gills – an action reputed to drive away all but the great white shark – had yet to be tested. Here, in open sea we felt vulnerable especially since we were unable to see what was beneath us and we were advertising our presence.

I understood that sharks can detect the vibrations of moving fish from several miles away so presumably the vibrations of the yacht travel much further. Add to this the trail of refuse – though sharks aren't fussy and swallow bottles, cans and human waste; a bored shark or hungry shark would find the temptation of a pair of threshing limbs irresistible. However, everyone made the buoys and there were no fins slicing the surface of the water.

Soon it was our turn. I watched Tim dive over the side rail and plunge into a soapy well which swallowed his legs. I stood for a while contemplating the distance to the water and the staying power of my bikini. If I dived I stood to lose both halves. If I jumped the bottom would be forced on and I could strategically position each hand to keep the top in place. I stepped over the rail and dropped rather than jumped conscious of the water both rushing to meet me and rushing past me. After the explosive impact I went down and up like a yo-yo surfacing to see the tow rope and Tim on a par with me. By working my way hand over hand along the rope I made for the space between the last two buoys. At first, hanging on was like being dragged along on a failed ski-lift but I knew I mustn't let go. Then I relaxed letting my body trail in the threshing water – a powerful and stimulating imitation of a Jacuzzi and, in retrospect, inviting bait for a hungry shark.

Back on deck there was a wonderful sense of well-being, inside as well as out. Everyone was relaxed: David and Anna settled down to a game of scrabble; Madge was sunning herself and immersed in Stephen King; Phil was studying *A Cruising Guide To The Philippines* and, Tim, at the helm, was amusing and distracting people with his anecdotes.

I don't remember most of Tim's stories – not because they are not worth remembering, I just don't remember stories, especially long ones. In fact Tim is a good storyteller. He has a natural talent for retelling what he's heard so that his version is invariably more amusing and colourful than the original. He also remembers a great deal of what he's read and conveniently functions as a walking encyclopaedia. This can be very useful when exploring a tropical island and you want to identify trails in the sand or if, like now, you are in the middle of The South China Sea and want to know how flying fish fly.

'They don't,' Tim explained, 'they glide – their propulsion is gained first, by an initial spurt to leave the water and then by dipping the extended lower lobe of the tail into the surface and finning like maniacs until they take off.'

Somehow the conversation shifted to the word 'posh' and Tim was explaining its origin from when the first British passenger ships sailed to and from the East.

'Upper class or genteel passengers, like Adrienne – before she met me,' he added, pausing to make sure he caught my eye – 'they were allocated cabins on the port side going out and on the starboard side on the way home: in theory to enjoy the shaded part of the ship on both journeys. Hence POSH: Port Out Starboard Home.'

I was half-listening, half-dreaming and gazing across the expanse of hummocky ocean. Just then I thought I saw a bird flying very fast and about a foot over the waves, then there were two, three, four –

not birds but flying fish. It was a remarkable sight: electric-blue fish, about six inches long, propelling themselves across the waves. I had never seen so many or at such close range. It was as if they had heard us talking and were here to demonstrate their technique, but their speed was such that it was impossible to detect how they travelled. We decided that they were probably flying to escape a predator. Perhaps we had attracted a shark after all.

I'd done my homework and knew that the Mako (killer) Shark can travel at sixty mph. I imagined the shadow of a Great White Shark, the same length as the *Star*, cruising beneath us terrifying the flying fish that were still shooting like missiles across the waves. Then contemplated the irony of flying fish who fly to escape underwater enemies only to find new enemies above the water – whether the deck of a boat where they sometimes stunned themselves, or the clutches of a waiting frigate bird.

For the rest of the day there was no other sign of life: just sea and sky and white sails holding back the sun. I began to wonder if the rest of the world existed.

Afternoon drifted into evening. Sails were flying; the dying sun had set the sky on fire: a perfect backdrop for sundowners. A large ship cropped the horizon and seemed to be heading in the same direction as us. We were in the Palawan Passage, a recommended safe shipping route, especially during the N-E Monsoon. In reality there is no such thing as safe sailing in this stretch of the South China Sea. For a start it's alive with guyots and oceanic islands formed by volcanic activity, as well as splendid coral reefs which, although paradise for divers, are lethal for sailors. I knew that the Palawan Passage averages twelve nautical miles in width and runs parallel to the western coast of the elongated island. To the east, towards the rugged coastline, the area is riddled with charted dangers but to the west the huge expanse of ocean is sparsely marked with a handful of scattered banks and shoals. The following printed warning appeared on our Admiralty chart:

DANGEROUS GROUND (See Caution)

The large area north-westwards of the recommended track is known to abound with dangers. No systematic surveys have been carried out and the existence of uncharted patches of coral and shoals is likely; the position of charted banks and shoals cannot be relied upon. Vessels are warned not to attempt to pass through this area.

The intriguing names of the unreliable and widely dispersed charted banks and shoals west of the passage played on my imagination. Perhaps they were unreliable because they were discovered through misadventure. 'Lord Auckland Shoals' suggested discovery by a stately figure, dressed like Nelson, standing on the bows of his grounded ship surveying the scene through a telescope. Whereas, 'Seahorse Bank' conjured a wildly romantic and mythical scene: a gathering of winged seahorses, taking off from the banks in a thunder of spray, pulling Neptune in their wake. Further to the north-west the isolated 'Marie Louise' was evocative of a ghostly deserted ship or a ship plundered by tidy cut-throat pirates.

Unfortunately, today's pirates are neither romantic nor mythical adventurers in the South China Sea. Piracy, like head-hunting, has a long history in South-East Asia. In the 16th Century the fearful Ilanuan and Balini Tribes from the Southern Philippines engaged in brutal and ferocious attacks against the infidel which began when Christian Spaniards captured Manila in 1570. For local people piracy was a means of self-defence and a legitimate way of making a living approved of by princes and sultans who derived a considerable part of their income from the proceeds of piratical activities. In the 19th

Century pirates fiercely resisted the exploratory expeditions of James Brooke and fellow colonisers.

The Illustrated London News, dated 24th April, 1852 gives an account of an attack on the crew of Her Majesty's Ship *'Royalist'* engaged in a survey of the island of Palawan *'a country but little known'*. The crew, returning from land exploration and making their way up the Malampaya Sound to the *'Royalist'* were approached by five large *prahus* (canoe-like boats), carrying from fifty to sixty men,

'exhibiting formidable appearance, advanced by open order in the form of a crescent, apparently with the intention of hemming us in.'

Fortunately, for the crew, when the attack was launched the shots fell wide and they escaped. It is further reported that *'both on the east and west coasts of Palawan, the people are kept in constant dread of them'*.

Much of the island of Palawan, especially the interior, is still *'a country but little known'* and to this day pirates instil fear in local fishermen, pleasure sailors and crews from small trading craft and large international vessels alike. As I had already discovered, accounts of these incidents can be read with increasing frequency in Singapore's 'Straits Times' – as well as in the local press in Brunei. The London based International Maritime Bureau reported 200 attacks in South-East Asia in 1992, along just one stretch of ocean, compared with 60 in 1990 and only three in 1989. Fortunately, it wasn't until we returned from the trip that I learnt about some of the more frightening attacks.

One of the most horrifying occurred off Mindoro Island north of Palawan. Some fisherman on a raft were beheaded, their bodies discarded and their heads tied like buoys to their fishing nets. There appeared to be no other motives other than sickening violence and a macabre gratification in the discovery of their massacre. The utter pointlessness of the atrocity was characteristic of the Camucones, ferocious predators of the Archipelago in the 17th Century. All Spaniards who fell into their hands were beheaded and their skulls used as drinking vessels. At least the head-hunters of Borneo had a motive for collecting their trophies: believing the head to be the location of the spirit they collected them to add powerful magic to their longhouses.

A week after our return I read about the latest weapon used for attack: petrol bombs. Memories of hair raising encounters on islands off the coast of Sabah, with my two daughters, were still with me; the thought of attack by pirates wielding cutlasses, parangs or guns was bad enough – attack by petrol bombs terrifying, especially on a fibreglass boat like the *Star of Siam*. In the reported incident petrol bombs had been hurled at a Malaysian international container ship when it tried to outrun the pirates' fast boat. On another occasion, also reported by The International Maritime Bureau, shortly after our return, pirates who fired at a ship while preparing to board received the shock of their lives when the ship returned fire with several rounds of artillery. The pirates, operating off the Philippines, hurriedly withdrew. They had unwittingly picked on a Russian warship: *Nikolai Vikov*.

The dilemma of patrolling and controlling international waters remains especially when it is so easy for pirates to escape into neighbouring foreign water without jurisdiction over them.

On this golden evening, joined by playful dolphins, the possibility of attack seemed remote.

Day 4

It was two a.m. and our fears about sea-pirates had returned. Tim was convinced we were being pursued by a pirate boat. Although it is difficult to estimate distance and speed at night, it was getting closer and looked as if it were on a deliberate collision course. It was near enough for us to distinguish the outline of a typical boat from the region of northern Sabah: high curving prow, a tall mast-like structure – but heavier and leaning towards the stern – probably a crane for hauling in fishing nets, and a square framework on deck used for living, sleeping and gutting fish.

Tim kept watch while I scanned the chart. There were no shoals to attract fishing boats marked in the region and from the deck there were no other fishing boats to be seen. We could think of no valid reason for the boat's course and, if they were pirates, apart from diving knives and cooking implements, we had no weapons to deter them or defend ourselves. We decided to turn out the lights and alter course in an attempt to lose them. We watched anxiously for a change in their direction. Very slowly the outline of the boat became less distinct and its lights dimmed until it was swallowed by darkness and we were alone once more.

The sky was startlingly clear. Among the plethora of stars the Southern Cross was the most brilliant and awe-inspiring. Visibility was so remarkable that stars just five degrees off the horizon were visible. Tim pointed out Polaris, usually visible only from much higher in the northern hemisphere than our seven degrees north. At 3.30 a.m. weary and with pirates still in mind, we saw a curved golden sail appear on the horizon. It had a luminous ghostly quality, like an apparition from the 'Ancient Mariner'. As we watched, it slowly lifted until it was floating in the sky. Then it became clear that it was neither a ghost ship nor astral phenomenon but the crescent moon – as gold as the sun.

Breakfast-time brought more excitement. Our tales about last night's sightings had fired everyone's imagination. Madge was busy scrambling eggs for breakfast when Phil spotted a boat heading towards us. Pirates, we decided, fearing that this time we wouldn't be so lucky. The vessel was steadily gaining on us and continued until it was close enough for them to identify the number and size of our crew. Fortunately our male contingent was bigger than average even by Western standards.

From across the waves, bearded and with long curly hair, Tim probably looked like a formidable pirate – both he and Phil are well over six feet. Although David didn't match the others in height, he was a keen sportsman and archery practice had done wonders for his biceps. Bronze and stripped to the waist he gave a passable impression of Tarzan. On the skipper's orders, the female contingent was lying low. Apart from Madge, who boasted a black belt in karate, we had no Amazonian qualities to make us worthwhile opposition. On the contrary, Tim assured us, female crew were bait, 'especially those with bare limbs,' he said, looking at Madge's short shorts and bikini top and my sarong behaving like a sail in the wind.

'Below deck!' he ordered.

Some minutes later I was edging up the galley steps to get a glimpse of our pursuers.

'Get down!' Tim called. 'You're lethal, blonde hair, white skin – there'll be no stopping them! And a tan's no disguise,' he continued anticipating my retort.

Whatever their criteria or interests, from what the possible pirates had seen, we didn't meet them for they suddenly altered course and headed east in the direction of land. Excitement over we tucked into cold scrambled eggs, pumpernickel bread – still edible after four days in the cool box – and mugs of coffee.

Mid-morning brought the customary drop in wind, and it looked as if we were set for another day of blue-water cruising: no land, no boats, no birds and no flying fish – even an earlier sighting of dolphins had deserted us. Shades of the 'Ancient Mariner' came back to me. Without the engine we too would have been: *as idle as a painted ship'*. Calm weather brought its compensations: we weren't going anywhere very fast but habitable deck-space was extended. An endless vista of ocean, white sails stretched against blue sky, swathes of spray catching rainbows. I drifted in and out of a trance-like state.

Meanwhile, Madge had finished washing and decorating the ship's rails with her entire wardrobe and was stretched out in the sun with Stephen King. David was dividing his time between fishing and playing scrabble with Anna while bemoaning the fact that he could have been improving his archery skills at Club Med. His lack of success with his fishing rod – he'd caught nothing but lost two hooks – became the butt of a series of jokes especially when, during a night-watch, he was hit on the head by a flying fish.

This was just one of several that landed on deck. The best catch was made by Anna when one became inadvertently trapped between her toes. Unfortunately, none survived, but we did have the opportunity to have a close look at their tiny webbed fins and the extended lower tail. Today, only the *Star* was flying and kept on course by Tim and Phil. At eleven a.m. I spotted a coconut husk bobbing past and felt as excited as if I were Noah when he sighted the dove carrying a leafy branch. Tim estimated another twenty-four hours to Bacuit Bay.

As day progressed wind and waves increased. The galley and cabins were beginning to look like the wreck of the Hesperus. There was little ice left and the remaining perishable food was starting to smell, as were the rubbish bags stacked behind the galley steps. In the afternoon I was catching up on some sleep in the forward cabin when a sudden deluge of cold water swamped me. Struggling to my feet and attempting to maintain my balance on the swaying berth I tried to close the hatch; it fell clamping my arm in its metal jaw. The scene on deck was all too familiar: the boat heeling with taff-rails in the water; bedraggled crew trying to keep in their seats; waves crashing over the deck and cascading over the windward side into the cockpit. Abandoned by Madge, Stephen King was looking damp and downtrodden while David, at the wheel, was doing an impression of a stork by standing on one leg and keeping his balance by propping the other against the adjacent seat.

It was at times like this, when everyone was crowded in the inadequate shelter of the cockpit, that even making a cup of tea assumed traumatic proportions. I'm a confessed caffeine addict and drink either tea or coffee at regular intervals. The galley is in full view of the cockpit and it seemed impolite and even churlish not to ask if anyone wanted to join me. They usually did. This meant putting sufficient water in the kettle for six people which would take at least twenty minutes to boil on the ineffectual gas burner. Then I took orders: tea or coffee – black or white – with or without sugar? Next I had to locate and wash six mugs. Meanwhile I was doing my utmost to remain upright and sweat was trickling down every crevice as if there were a leak on top of my head.

Half an hour later, operation complete and clutching my mug of tea, I staggered up the galley steps into the cockpit; with just enough room on each bench for three people to sit side by side it resembled the crowded, open upper-deck of a bus in a flood. Next, mug of tea in one hand, I had to maintain my balance while climbing over several pairs of knees – trying not to scald them in the process – and then squeeze into my favourite spot in the back corner of the stern. After four days and four nights my earlier fears of confinement were beginning to override my expectations of the thrill of adventure.

Just as I was beginning to feel mildly suicidal I spotted a pale grey outline on the horizon. Slowly it grew more distinct and there was more of it. I entertained a horrible fear that it was heavy cloud and we were sailing into a storm. Then Phil, who had been plotting our position, fell up the galley steps. According to Satnav we were approaching the coast of Palawan. I didn't really care if it were Palawan or if we had crossed the sea to China. It was land. It was static. To my dismay Tim announced that in order to reach land we had to tack out to sea again. We were already sailing as close to the wind as we could and the only way forward was backwards or, at least, sideways. Light was failing and before long the pale hills had dissolved behind us. Predictably, rough weather, excessive heat and darkness colluded in time for the evening meal.

The traumas I suffered making tea were pale compared with those experienced cooking the evening meal. The avuncular nature of the skipper meant there was no strict duty rota. In fact there was no rota. He assumed that if someone was working it was because they wanted to. Madge's need for food had much the same result as my need for caffeine. She did most of the cooking, at least during the first few days of the trip. The 'rest' she had been looking forward to was not materialising. Paired with Phil for sailing and domestic duties, as and when they arose, she was clearly irritated by his domestic failings. As far as the evening meal was concerned I was just as guilty. I preferred to eat bread and cheese or go without rather than suffer in the galley.

As the trip progressed, Anna came to the rescue, assisted and hindered by David she concocted some spicy dishes served with generous portions of noodles or glutinous rice. David was in the habit of hovering behind Anna as she cooked commenting, correcting and occasionally taking over. This evening he hovered, littering his comments with 'Honey' – a reciprocal term they appeared to use instead of first names, except when angry. I supposed there were levels of anger for, at times, the tone used for 'Honey' was clearly not one of affection. Now, David was in full flow:

'Keep stirring, Honey – Honey, I told you – keep the flame low – just a touch more cumin, Honey. Here,' he added, taking the saucepan from her, 'let me!'

Apart from nondescript grunting sounds in her throat Anna made no response to the catalogue of instructions. The cooking done David took on the role of master-chef and tasted the carefully spiced main dish.

'Not enough salt, Honey,' he said, shaking a damp packet of salt over it. As several lumps fell into the pan a mildly explosive Anna could be heard remonstrating from below.

Even the memory of mouth-watering spicy smells wafting from the galley during preparation could not override the fact that Anna's carefully prepared dish tasted of nothing but salt. Served with a solid mass of glutinous rice it was a disaster. We ate in silence. I picked at mine for a respectable length of time then glad of the darkness donated the contents of my plate to the hungry sea.

Day 5

Dawn-watch is a gift. It is even worth the agony of being wrenched from sleep. At four a.m. someone was tugging my foot as if it were a door-pull. I sat up and switched to automatic pilot, moving like a robot but feeling like a trampled sponge. I lived and slept in sarongs so I didn't have the problem of finding and struggling into clothes. Meanwhile Tim was everything I wasn't: alert, cheerful, practical and in control. He checked and plotted our position and took control of the wheel. I made the tea. After two mugs I began to feel vaguely human and responsible. By this time Tim was beginning to wilt. I took the wheel while he stretched out. Seconds later he was asleep but within shaking distance in case of rocks, pirates or astral phenomena.

This was the time I loved best. I, alone, was awake, the wheel in my hands, surrounded by ocean and under a canopy of stars. The sails were full; there was no sound except shushing waves breaking over the prow. The sky was electric. Even the Milky Way's distant, nebulous stars were sparkling like frost. Then, like an action replay, I watched a golden sail slip over the horizon: the sky was lit by the luminescent light of the rising sun, heralding the new day. As she rose, the sky turned sugar-almond pink and there, haloed by an aura of shot gold, were the outlines of distant mountains.

Tim woke. I made more tea. We were sailing towards the now mushrooming mountains and heading for Mayday Bay. It was suitably named for the area is riddled with reefs, shoals, islands and headlands. We identified the pointed tip of Cleopatra's Needle – at 5,000 feet the highest visible peak – and were fascinated by the wild and suggestive names of our craggy surroundings – among them, Conical Point, Native Point, Intercourse Point, Perforated Point and Savage Island: names that questioned Palawan's title of 'Land of Beautiful Harbours'. Then Tim announced a change of plan – our first stop was to be Port Barton – a few hours away. We were all longing for land under our feet and fresh supplies of ice, food and fuel were becoming urgent. Neither the supplies nor the crew would benefit from the extra sailing time needed to reach Bacuit Bay as previously planned. I was dreaming about eating at a fixed table; Tim was imagining ice-cold San Miguel beer. Meanwhile, at 4.5 knots, we were heading directly into the sun, across sea as smooth as a satin counterpane, towards growing mountains.

It was tantalising to see land but know that we still had several hours sailing ahead of us. We watched a huge Filipino naval vessel on the same heading come up from behind, overtake and streak ahead. Just then Phil spotted a huge jet of water spouting into the air some distance away to our port-side. 'Could be a whale,' he said, rummaging for his binoculars and showing more excitement than he had shown so far on the trip. Then we spotted a boat some hundred metres away from the spot and heard a muffled explosion followed by another jet of water.

'That's no whale,' Tim responded. 'They're detonating coral – trying to save fishing time.'

We contemplated sailing closer to identify and report the vessel but as well as the danger of being blown to pieces with the coral, they could disappear faster than we could approach and we still had a couple of hours tricky navigation through dangerous reefs before we arrived. Helped by Phil as navigator and an unexpected lift in wind, Tim steered clear of dangers and we made good progress. Mountains and rocks that moments ago had resembled sleeping dinosaurs were rushing towards us, sprouting rocks and trees.

We anchored in a curved turquoise bay a few hundred metres from the beach, surrounded by mountains and islands. A thickly wooded hill, cresting a plantation of coconut palms, appeared to be nudging them towards the sea. Directly in front of us was Swissippinni Cottage – outstanding for its size and style: a rectangular, two-storey, pseudo-Swiss building laced with galleys and ornate wooden balustrades. The Swiss owner's use of a combination of Filipino and Alpine features worked remarkably well, especially since both depended entirely on the use of wood. In contrast to the more modern and stylish architecture of Swissippinni Cottage the nearby settlement's wooden stilt houses, straggling beneath leggy palms, must have looked much the same as when

Frank Barton, the American naval officer, discovered and named the place nearly one hundred years ago.

The most striking features of the bay were the colourful fishing boats. Hewn out of tree trunks and painted in bright blues and greens they reflected the brilliant kingfisher hues of the water. Two bamboo outriggers, running parallel to each side and of the same length, were held just above the water by three curved cross-poles. Fixed to the hull these provided lateral stability and were a distinctive feature of Filipino boats. An awning erected at one end gave shelter from fierce tropical sun while a crossed pole – a mast with a light attached – resembled a crucifix. The boats were big enough to house a large family and although they used diesel power instead of sails and paddles, they otherwise appeared identical in design to the ubiquitous fighting ships used by their ancestors in the 17th Century.

Finally, we were on land though it was far from static. The swaying sensation of the boat remained with us for some time. We trudged drunkenly across the beach, the sun behind us, the air thrumming with heat and vibrant with the shrill of cicadas.

Port Barton, slotted between the backdrop of hills and sea, consists of a settlement of stilt houses divided into rows by three parallel sandy tracks – the main roads – which are criss-crossed by smaller paths leading to the beach. The walls of the rickety houses are made up from panels woven from coconut leaves – the fronds, placed side by side – and the overlapping leaves interwoven. The ridged central spines serve as support columns. The overall design is rather like herringbone tweed. The roof is made in a similar way except that the fronds are doubled in half along the spines and the leaves from each side are woven together forming a thick fringe. A succession of these is laid across the outer roof framework so that they overlap and serve as waterproof thatching.

Repairs to the houses are haphazard: an extra pole propped under a falling wall and tied with coconut fibre; patches that don't fit. I supposed that when rain did come in, it drained out just as easily, and if the house blew down during a typhoon no-one would be seriously hurt by collapsing timber and it would be relatively simple and inexpensive to put it together again. On the other hand those houses beyond repair, like the discarded boats lying on the beach and in the muddy estuary, are left to disintegrate into the vegetation, sand or mud until they are reabsorbed into the natural cycle of decay and growth.

Walking through the sandy streets was like walking backwards through time. Torpid heat and a sense of timelessness were all-pervading. Men, women and children stood about in small groups talking and watching. The most popular pastime appeared to be head-hunting for lice. Stray dogs and cockerels wandered about scratching, pecking or dozing in the shade. Tethered, fierce-looking pigs, bloated with fat, sprawled and wallowed in hot sand. A huge black specimen opened one eye and gave a half-grunt/half-snuffle as I warily approached to take a photograph. In the middle of a patch of swampy ground a water pump was the centre of female activity – women and girls squatting in the mud enjoying bath-time and washday.

Apart from the occasional moped the only road transport we saw was a brightly decorated Jeepney – a mini-bus used to cross the mountains to reach Roxas on the east coast. When the Americans moved out of the Philippines, following the liberation from the Japanese in 1945, one of their legacies was a fleet of jeeps. Adopted by the Filipinos, they converted them into a form of mass transport known as Jeepneys.

In Palawan, Jeepneys were the only mode of transport used to reach Roxas and the capital, Puerto Princesa. Every inch was flamboyantly decorated. The more avant-garde versions display saintly figures of the Virgin and Child side by side with blond pinups, tropical flowers, fish and graffiti, plus accessories in the form of lights, streamers, tassels, amulets and icons covering the windows; turn on the stereo and the Jeepney becomes a fair on wheels. Inside there is seating for ten people in two rows, facing each other. Between the rows of knees a cargo of chickens, blocks of melting ice, pigs, sacks of rice and cans of diesel complete the travelling roadshow.

The street nearest the beach seemed to be the main shopping area. Some of the houses had been converted into stores and sold goods ranging from hands of bananas and fresh mangoes to plastic kitchen wear, sun creams and cosmetics and best of all, fresh bread. We replaced our lost bucket, bought fruit and bread and finally tracked down a boatman who offered to get supplies of fuel if we were prepared to wait till the next day. It would take him three to four hours both ways by Jeepney to collect fuel from Roxas. We could expect it by late morning. By Filipino standards this could mean a couple of days. We decided to stay overnight and with luck leave for Bacuit Bay before sunset the following day. We learnt that ice could be ordered from Swissippinni Cottage – this, too, would be transported from Roxas.

Swissippinni Cottage turned out to be a haven for travellers: open plan with comfortable cane furniture, a bar, restaurant, its own generator to keep overhead fans spinning and, for us, a view across the bay to the *Star of Siam*. As if that wasn't enough there was the additional luxury of showers. The thought of a fresh water shower was almost as good as the thought of the cold beers we had just ordered. Over glasses of San Miguel we examined the impressive menu: apart from '*LAPU-LAPU or other first-class fish in creamy white sauce*', there was a range of seafood and meat dishes, and a choice of vegetables and wines. Our excitement was short-lived. The evening meal was restricted to what was available which would be served as a buffet. We ordered food and another round of beers. I decided to beat the rush to the showers.

Modern by Port Barton's standards, the washing-block was brick built and housed two showers, two loos – one with a closet and seat and one with the traditional hole in the ground – and an area with a sink for washing clothes large enough to keep even Madge happy for hours. The decidedly phallic shower-head jutted from the wall about a foot above my head. I undressed and turned on the tap. Nothing – but I could hear water splashing next door. I waited. The splashing stopped and a trickle of water oozed from the spout over my head. This slowly gathered momentum until it resembled the thin stream from *Manneken Pis*. The sheer luxury of salt free water compensated for the lack of momentum.

Back on the Star we were just in time to watch the sun disappear behind the mountains. Tim was making our first radio contact with an enterprising friend who has his own radio station in Kuala Belait. I poured two G and Ts, left one on the chart table and went on deck. Orange light flooded the sky and spread across the sea. One by one lights around the bay came on casting reflections in the water. The chorus of cicadas reached a crescendo and was broken by the sound of a boat chugging by – then it appeared: a black silhouette slipping out from the bay. Night was the time of activity as, one by one, fishing boats' bobbing lights crossed the bay making for the shoals and a night's work.

Day 6

The sea was striped bands of turquoise, lapis lazuli, emerald, tourmaline – long shadows from the palm trees stretched across the beach, cloud shadows quilted sleepy hills, a cock crowed. Morning had arrived.

Breakfast at Swissippinni Cottage was followed by a leisurely day waiting for deliveries of fuel and ice. We left David alternately teasing and feeding two caged monkeys. When they weren't filling their pouches with bananas they were snatching at David's hair. Meanwhile he was directing Anna, who was behind the camera.

'Move back, Honey. Wait till he grabs my hair! Use the zoom! No, not that button, Honey.'

Resisting the temptation to free the monkeys to grab as much of David's hair as they wanted I left him to his antics and adopting the unhurried, unworried mentality of the Filipinos joined Madge for a stroll along the beach. Still shaded by palm trees it was the focus of activity: children played among boats and fishing nets, adults squatted in the shade or tended to their boats. There was a sudden flurry of excitement. A sack running along the beach and pursued by several laughing boys, rolled over and squealed: a pig in a poke. We watched the boys catch the wriggling sack, drag it unceremoniously along the sand and sling it onto a boat already dangerously overloaded with people. Deciding that I could well end up on a spit in its place, I quelled thoughts about rescuing the captive pig. Then a ginger-haired bespectacled male was hurrying down the beach towards us, dabbing the sweat from his face with the end of his shirt.

'Any chance of a lift?' he asked catching up and falling into step. 'You are from the yacht?' he continued gesturing towards the Star. 'I hear you're going to El Nido.'

We gave him the same 'Sorry. Full House,' reply we'd given some German backpackers we met last evening over the buffet. The unlucky traveller made off the way he had come still dabbing at his red face. Apart from an American woman, on leave from a teaching job in Japan, backpackers appeared to be the only other visitors in

Port Barton. They had two means of travel: local pump boat or Jeepney, unless they were lucky enough to find a yacht willing to take them and, unless the skipper was in need of extra crew, this was unlikely. One of the Germans, wearing a cotton sun-hat several sizes too small, a floral shirt and shorts was sitting reading a book, his feet in the advancing surf.

Then a sudden bout of activity was provided by the arrival of the crew of the Filipino naval vessel that had overtaken us on our approach to the bay. Averaging five feet in height and dressed in long shorts and heavy boots a group of them were soon in hot pursuit of white flesh. There was a limited supply. We declined their offers of rides in boats to deserted islands and bottles of champagne but nothing was going to deter them. Finally, entourage in tow, we made for the place where Tim and Phil were supervising the arrival of the fuel. Madge pointed to them,

'Our husbands,' she said, 'they'll be very angry if they see us talking to you!'

She was convincing and effective. They stopped in their tracks, examined the supposed husbands then wandered back the way they had come. Madge confirmed my belief that the only repellent for persistent males in the East is a husband, especially a tall bearded one. Nevertheless, I made a mental note to take up karate.

Day 7

A range of mountains and islands grew out of thinning darkness. As we moved into the bay, ragged silhouettes wrapped round us. The sun peeled into orange sky spreading a rosy sheen across the water. As the intensity of light increased detail leafed from rugged islands: wooded slopes and small white coves – emerald strips and patches bloomed in the sea over reefs of coral. We were heading for

Pangalusian Island and Jock Gordon's place. Jock Gordon is a well-known figure in this part of the world. An ex-sailor he married, Becky, a Filipino girl, built his dream house on a tropical island and sadly became terminally ill and died. Since Jock's death two years ago, Becky has continued to run the place as a guest-house for sailors, divers and travellers – Jacques Cousteau is said to be one of the more distinguished names in the visitors' book.

'That's it,' said Tim, 'that's Jock's dream.'

We were approaching one of several paradisiacal islands; a white house was set in the curve of a bay just a few metres from the beach and sheltered, from behind, by a hill. The thatched, many sided, central building looked circular from a distance. Behind it the outline of a craggy hill was silhouetted against cerulean sky as clear as the water. The house was surrounded by flowering shrubs: bright orange and cerise bougainvillea, exotic yellow fist-sized blooms, sweet-smelling pink and white frangipani.

The thunder of the falling anchor-chain woke the rest of the crew. Leaving them to drink tea and take in the idyllic surroundings, I set off with Tim to make arrangements for an evening meal. It was not yet seven a.m. but we had seen movement around the house. Since we were anchored on the edge of a reef we had to navigate the dinghy over coral that, at times, was no more than a few centimetres from the surface. Through pellucid water there was a perfect view into an underwater world bright with multi-coloured, multi-shaped fish and coral. As we neared the beach the water was plagued with small, brown, pulsating jellyfish. Stranded specimens littered the sand like clumps of seaweed.

A wooden porchway led into a huge circular room, flanked on either side by a wide sweeping staircases leading to a gallery. A bar was the central feature of the room. Over it and under the engraved words: Kencho (Dragon) Bar, was a huge driftwood dragon, painted gold. Unfortunately, Becky was in Manila for a few days but her brother, John, made us welcome.

The multi-purpose gallery – some twelve feet wide – was open on both sides and furnished with wooden dining tables and chairs. One side looked over the island and the other down to the bar. From the opposite side a walkway led to a look-out platform where an old ship's mast, similar to that of the *Star* tapered into the sky: a hallmark and memento to Jock and his sailing days. Around us stretched a panorama of sea and scattered islands. Below humming-birds hovered over waxy blooms; huge butterflies wafted here and there as if in a dream. Over coffee we ordered dinner: lobster, crab, giant prawns and salad.

'Seven o'clock or thereabouts?' Tim asked.

'Or whenever the lobsters arrive,' replied John his black eyes creasing into a smile.

'We have to catch them first!'

By mid-morning: there was enough wind to sail round the islands and Tim promised us a mystery tour. We were heading for an isolated rock. As we approached its dark sides grew out of the waves like the hunched shoulders of a wading giant. We dropped anchor at a safe distance and one by one Tim took us to explore. From the dinghy the massive craggy outcrop towered and leant over us. Swifts darted in and out of crevices and fissures; a startled heron took off, streaking across the ruffled mirror of sea. As we drew near the waves became choppy and the menacing sound of water trapped and struggling in dark hollows rang and echoed. A Gothic entrance led into a flooded cave as dark as it was cold. My eyes were lifted by light streaming through an overhead crater like shafts of light from a window. Gradually as my eyes adjusted to the darkness I could make out shapes resembling cloaked figures on the rock walls: great, smooth vertical ridges and folds towered over us like those on the sculptured walls of a great cathedral.

Next on our agenda was to find a perfect place for a picnic. Surrounded by islands with white sandy coves and the pre-requisite palm trees we were spoilt for choice. Our greatest problem was that each time we made a decision we were already sailing by the chosen spot. Finally, we pinpointed an island straight ahead of us, sailed to the edge of a fringe of coral, dropped the anchor, packed the cool-box, made two trips in the dinghy and were there.

We had found the perfect picnic place but the contents of the hurriedly packed cool-box had not survived transportation. The kettle of drinking water had spilled and everything, including all the remaining tea-bags we had on board, was floating. My mission was to salvage the dripping tea-bags. Ignoring Tim's protests that there would be nothing left except tannin I rescued them, one by one, by their yellow and red Lipton's labels and placed them on a rock to dry. This accomplished I helped Madge collect driftwood for the fire. David, busy practising his boy-scout fire-lighting skills with soggy matches, was producing enough smoke to match a forest fire while Phil was making brave attempts at domesticity by wrapping potatoes in foil to be baked or smoked. Since David's promise of fish for the barbecue did not materialise we substituted with tinned tuna. Tim was adding a creative touch by mixing tuna with sweetcorn and mayonnaise with one hand while distributing cans of warm beer with the other.

While the potatoes were baking I wandered along the beach and climbed over some rocks to the adjoining cove. It was more picturesque than our beach, much wider and splashed with vibrant red and orange blooms of wild bougainvillea growing up the cliff side. Someone had already discovered the beach and staked a claim. There were two thatched beach huts but no sign of life. The sand was decorated with monkey trails – toed footprints and a straight runnel from the dragging tail which distinguishes them from the lizard's clawed feet and winding tail marks. Nearer the sea the sand was decorated by shells and the perfectly executed repetitive tank-tracks of hermit crabs.

I was walking along the frill of waves collecting shells when I stopped short. There, in front of me, about one metre from the water's edge, was the elliptical shell of a giant turtle – its body and head buried in the sand. Was it asleep? Hibernating? Laying eggs? Curiosity overcame me. I leant across the dome, put my fingers under the rim of the shell and tried to lift it. At first it wouldn't budge, then very slowly its great weight began to shift. Suddenly, there was the sensation of tearing, the weight falling away and waves of heat and energy as from the open door of a heated oven. The shell lifted clear of the sand nearly throwing me off-balance. It was hollow except for a neat column of spinal bones, intact and following the centre of the dome from end to end. Huge flaps of thick leathery skin with fingered ends hung on either side. The sensation of heat, now accompanied by a pungent smell came from the sandy compost heap of rotting flesh and guts, writhing with maggots and decorated with bones. I lowered the shell to cover the open grave and to the quench the smell of decay.

I wanted to keep the shell but knew I would meet a barrage of disapproval, even from Tim. In spite of wry comments in the vein of ' Why can't you collect stamps like normal people,' he was tolerant of my penchant for collecting huge pieces of driftwood in Brunei – sculptured remains of massive buttress roots – and even helped me by transporting them from the beach to the verandah of my abode in his 4WD. However, I knew he wouldn't agree to a ripe turtle shell on board even if we cut the flaps of skin away and scoured it in the sea.

It was early evening when we reached Jock Gordon's place. The sun was low on the horizon – sky and sea were on fire. We estimated that by now the lobsters must have arrived and were probably well on their way to the table; Phil took on the role of ferryman. He dropped Madge, David and Anna and, just as the last embers of the sun were glowing behind the opposite chain of islands, returned for Tim and me. When we reached the shore the sky was deep amber and the water the colour of *Mouton Cadet,* making it impossible to detect lurking jellyfish. There was nothing for it but to wade as quickly and as purposefully as possible through the dark water, dragging the dinghy after us.

Dinner was served at a huge polished table on the look-out platform, under the stars. A dozen blazing torches – made from paraffin-filled San Miguel bottles slotted into the split heads of bamboo poles – fixed to the surrounding walls, created an Elizabethan atmosphere while two paraffin lamps, one at either end of the table, added to the authenticity of the place by attracting clouds of mosquitoes. Fortunately, someone had remembered the insect spray – the only perfume to wear in the tropics. Liberal applications were made to all exposed parts followed by our daily dosage of malaria pills. Then the food arrived: huge lobsters, crabs and prawns, a range of salads and various dishes of rice. For dessert – trays of fruit: watermelon slices, papaya, mangoes, pineapple, star-fruit. Every dish was decorated with fresh flowers. A banquet to remember and appreciated all the more after deprived gastronomic days at sea.

It was a perfect night: the air heavy with the fragrance of frangipani, the sky dusted with stars. A haunting cry echoed across the water; the frayed edges of waves shone like the luminous frills on a huge petticoat. This was to be an undisturbed night: horizontal berths – no night watches. As everyone prepared for sleep the *Star* creaked and groaned then settled into a gentle swaying rhythm. Our sky window was filled with stars. The lament of a bird rang into the night heralding a sudden lift of wind. It wafted through our sky-window and sent the boat into a steady swashing movement. We slipped into its rhythm becoming part of it, becoming part of the night.

Day 8

Mid-morning: we were heading for El Nido where the backdrop of cliffs is a dramatic example of the results of earth-shaking activity that continues throughout the Archipelago. The Philippine Islands – 7,000 of them – are part of the aptly named *Chain of Fire* – a line of volcanic activity that occurs where the Asian and Pacific Continental Plates converge. This line stretches from the Aleutian Islands to Japan, through the Philippines and Indonesia down to New Zealand. Fracture zones run the length of the Philippine Archipelago. Along these zones a variety of features, resulting from plate convergence are evident, of which the most extreme are twelve active volcanoes – most recently Mount Pinatubo, north of Manila on Luzon Island – and east of Mindanao Island: a deep open trench, the Mindanao Trough, plunges to 10,670 metres. Before us rose a magnificent vertical cliff wall that forms the fault scarp of the west coast of Northern Palawan.

From the chart it was possible to see that many of the smaller islands off Palawan were once part of the main island. The jigsaw shapes matched perfectly. From the sea vertical mountains looked like the side of a magnificent gorge or rift valley; those closest to us were split into segments resembling gigantic slates stacked neatly side by side. Some of the mountains' sheer vertical sides reached to 600 feet. Magnificent craggy heads continued to dominate the sky-line while at sea-level the rock walls had been severely undercut for several metres so that light could be seen under them and above the level of the water.

El Nido – The Nest – was so named because of its most valuable export of swifts' nests. Swift nest soup, made from the droppings and glutinous saliva swifts use to line and support their nests, is considered a delicacy by the Chinese. For centuries they have sailed across the South China Sea to the Philippines and Borneo to barter for this luxury.

Collecting the nests is a life-risking activity. At El Nido locals scale the vertical cliff-face to get at the nests lodged hundreds of meters high in cavities and fissures. In Sarawak's Niah Caves, families who have inherited the tradition, climb slender bamboo poles attached to the rock ceilings up to sixty metres from the ground; this enables them to keep their balance while scraping nests off the ceiling and helps them make a safe descent. On a visit to the Niah caves we could see the distant glow of flickering candles attached to the heads of the collectors as they worked high above us. As long ago as AD 700 the Niahians were trading hornbill ivory and edible birds' nests for Chinese porcelain and beads. Today, the tradition continues but the terms differ – the nests are sold for cash. A kilo of nests in Palawan will fetch over 300 pesos in local markets and a great deal more in Manila where *Nido Soup* along with *shark's fin soup* are served as traditional starters to meals in Chinese restaurants.

As we drew near, the settlement of El Nido – lodged at the foot of a magnificent cliff-wall – took shape. The centre of the town, marked by several buildings two and three storeys high, was flanked by rows of thatched stilt houses while the turquoise bay was like a busy aquatic parking area.

Although much bigger and more crowded, in overall design the town resembled Port Barton: three sandy roads parallel to the sea between houses and stores, criss-crossed by smaller tracks leading to the beach. The main street was lined with rows of two-storey, shoulder to shoulder houses separated by narrow alleys cluttered with refuse, stray dogs, cats and cockerels. Sticky heat, dust, flies and stagnant smells were intensified by the mid-day sun. The overhanging upper storeys of the houses with windows at eye-level, added to the Dickensian feel of the place. Through one window, partially covered by a tattered blind, I could see a wooden table and one chair. There were no other furnishings. On a pile of rags in a corner, someone was curled up asleep. A child was crying.

Outside, a faded poster advertised the forth-coming election in Manila. The Filipino political world of power, greed and violence centred in Manila seemed as incongruous as it was remote to this community of self-sufficient farmers and fishermen. As if to reinforce this sentiment, beyond and above the houses, the imposing and awesome vertical cliffs reared like the walls of an impenetrable fortress.

We were on the look out for overnight accommodation and fuel for our diving tanks. While Tim and I went in search of the locally based Bacuit Divers the others set off to find a pad for the night; with Tim leading the way we located the divers on the ground floor of a warehouse. Inside there was no light except what filtered through a grimy window overlooking an alley. As my eyes adjusted I could see a few masks and pairs of black flippers on a shelf, some badly chipped cylinders propped against a wall and, most importantly, a compressor to refuel our tanks. Fortunately, the place adjoined the beach so we arranged to take the dinghy back to the *Star* to collect then deliver the cylinders to the doorstep.

When we met up with the rest of the crew it was to discover that they had had no success in finding a suitable eating place, never mind accommodation. Of the two recommended – Bay View Hotel didn't exist and the only sign of hospitality offered by Elm Street Quarters was chalked on a board on the pavement: *Special Today –*

Spaghetti, wasn't on offer. In fact, the nightmare increased for by now we were hot, tired and hungry and when we finally found and roused the owner from his siesta, he informed us that not only was there no spaghetti but there was no food. Phil and Madge had already inspected and rejected a cafe over the warehouse adjoining Bacuit Divers but there was no choice.

We climbed the stairs, avoiding looking too closely at the kitchen just visible on the ground floor. The shabby room was cluttered with plastic chairs and tables and humming with flies. The choice of drinks was limited to canned pineapple or beer, and food to rice and fish. While we were waiting – it took fifteen minutes for the drinks to arrive and after thirty minutes there was still no sign or smell of food; meanwhile the ginger-haired backpacker we had encountered at Port Barton arrived.

'I wish I hadn't come now,' he said, swiping at a whirlpool of flies over his head. 'It's taken me over an hour to find this place and I don't know where I'm staying tonight.'

We knew the feeling but we also knew that we had the *Star* to return to. It was reassuring to look across the bay and see her bobbing among the Filipino boats. The food, when it came, was edible if not palatable and served the dual purpose of saving us from cooking a meal when we returned to the *Star* and passing the time taken to fill the cylinders.

Its dramatic setting apart, El Nido did not inspire and before the sun had set we were under sail. Massive heads of rock became silhouettes of gargoyles and monsters – mountain chains took on human shapes: a pregnant woman lying on her back; a Herculean man resting on his elbow reminiscent of Gulliver reclining in the sea off Lilliput. The sky behind them deepened from cyclamen pink to fiery orange. As we slipped out of the bay lights from a fleet of fishing boats sparkled like a constellation of stars.

Day 9

At dawn we were greeted by a similar scene to the one we had left last night: a semi-circle of lights from a fishing fleet but by now we had left Palawan behind and were heading for the southern end of the Calamian Islands. Lights from the fishing boats haloed the sky like rising moons. One by one they slipped over the horizon towards us forming a ring of blazing torches – their reflections picked up and repeated in ripples like strings of luminous beads. The sea was silk-smooth and so clear that stars were reflected as if in a mirror. Then the outlines of islands took shape, lower and less rugged than El Nido's cliffs with conical tops and dipping saddles between them. As we headed for Dicabaito Channel the sea became ruffled and full of strange eddies and whirls. We were caught in the beginning of the tidal rip where the South China Sea struggles to flow into the Sulu Sea. The *Star* rocked through the turbulent water until we were drawn into the channel between Dicabaito and Culion Islands.

The sea turned silvery blue then orange, reflecting bands of colour sweeping across the sky. We were heading directly into the rising sun. It was pure theatre – the drama enhanced by a backdrop of black low-lying islands fringed with gold. Like a slow motion film the bald tip of the sun's swollen head lifted flooding the sky first blood-red, then every variance of red, orange, gold. It was like watching an image thrown on an immense screen while someone with fingertip control changed the filters. As the sun cleared the islands, a carpet of brilliant gold unfurled across the ocean towards us, as ominous as it was exhilarating. Surrounded by glittering ocean and heading into a pathway of dazzling light that stretched between us and the horizon we were as blind as Paul on the road to Damascus. There was no voice from the sky but in the terms of Chinese geomancy we were heading towards disaster.

Chinese geomancers believe that Earth is a mirror of the Heavens shot through with energy lines. These can be positive lines carrying good *chi* or life-force, known as dragon-lines, or negative lines carrying bad *chi* from dangerous cross-currents. Good *chi* follows the directing magnetic fields beneath the Earth's surface – sometimes marked by underground rivers – and can be identified on the surface by uninterrupted views of treed mountain slopes. On the other hand bare rocks and scree and glittering water denote bad *chi*. Many Chinese still employ *feng shui:* wind and water experts to advise them before erecting a building or positioning a grave or bed so the object can be aligned with a dragon-line and shielded from dangerous cross-currents.

We were in a narrow channel between two dangerous shallow fringe reefs and with no option but to continue sailing directly into the path of 'malign' dazzling light. Tim was sailing by sight on an estimated position between the two islands. It was impossible to look ahead without sunglasses but with them it was difficult to see the edges of the coral. While sunglasses were essential for Tim, for my task: hanging over the taff-rails on the look out for the edge of the reef – it was easier to see beneath the glittering surface without glasses and by squinting against the glare.

The water's depth varied from twenty metres, in the narrow channel between two fringe reefs where we were sailing, to less than one meter over the coral on either side. Our problems were compounded by the temperamental depth-gauge which had stuck at thirty-four metres and the re-emergence of the turbulent tide race through the channel which was pushing us towards the shallow water. Suddenly, there was a resounding crunch and the *Star* lurched and groaned to a halt. We had mounted the reef edge. The rest of the bewildered crew, jarred unceremoniously from sleep, appeared on deck. Then to add insult to injury the Satnav alarm sounded. Our estimated position was the last thing we needed to know.

What we did need to know was the extent of the damage. Following Tim's instructions Phil checked for leaks below deck while David donned mask and fins and disappeared under water to assess the situation from outside. There were no obvious leaks inside and David could see nothing more than long scratches on the keel which was resting solidly on the top of the reef edge. Tim, who had remained quiet and thoughtful throughout, was now directing the proceedings for rescue. The kedge anchor was to be attached to a rope, taken in the dinghy, several meters beyond the edge of the reef, and dropped. Then by threading the other end of the rope through the end of the boom and winching it in we could wind the rope in until the line pulled us over at a sufficient angle to raise the keel. The theory was that with the boom pulled downwards away from the reef the boat would heel considerably, reducing the draught and we could then reverse clear using the engine.

Dressed in a sarong, a straw boater and dark glasses – looking more like a Club Med tourist than the invaluable sailor he was proving to be – David brought the dinghy round to the port side while Tim tethered the anchor. While they were pre-occupied I took the opportunity to take some photographs. Over the reef edge there was a black void. Sunlight glanced off the surface as if it were covered by a shiny impenetrable skin. On the starboard side through gin-clear water, less than a meter deep, the colour ranged through every nuance of blue and green between splendid heads of coral – a petrified world of huge sand-coloured flowers and fans. On one edge of the platform the outline of a statuesque seahorse looked down on the black hole which plummeted to a region of eternal night.

It was time to abandon my camera and join the human chain needed to slowly lower the anchor into the dinghy without tipping David out. This safely accomplished David dropped the anchor away from the reef edge. With the rope threaded through the boom and caught round the winch all we had to do was wind it in. A rather agitated Madge was trying to be part of every stage of the action. Phil was turning the winch and I was tailing the end of the rope, keeping it tightly bound as Phil wound. Just as he stopped winching and I was about to cleat the rope Madge grabbed hold, jerking it from my hands and losing the tension. It leapt from her careering backwards round the winch in crazy bursts. She made frantic efforts to regain control and suffering severe rope burns but without success. Phil came to the rescue. Madge disappeared into the galley.

Meanwhile Anna was relaying messages to and from David who had returned to the starboard side to monitor our progress. The *Star* was still firmly wedged. Tim switched on the engine and put it in reverse. Then miraculously the combined actions of the rope pulling us sideways and the engine thrusting us backwards worked – very slowly and deliberately the *Star* ground free. Our last task, to recover the anchor, was less successful. It had been dragged into the reef and would not budge. There was only one thing to do: cut the rope and lose the anchor. Anna was in position. Tim handed her his diving-knife and she set about severing the rope with alacrity.

With the sun overhead, highlighting pale turquoise strips and patches over sandy areas and with six pairs of eyes on the look-out for coral we passed safely through the remaining channel and moored in a sheltered inlet on the leeward side of Dicabaito Island. We discussed the possibility of diving to retrieve the anchor but decided that the ride back in the dinghy was too far; we could run out of fuel; our diving gear was heavy and we could capsize and, even if we located the anchor it was unlikely that we would be able to free and salvage it before our air ran out. Finally, showing unusual caution and revealing suppressed anxiety over the possible consequences of this morning's adventure, Tim concluded: 'To dive in that current is crazy. Fortunately we do have a spare.' We abandoned the idea. Instead Tim had an alternative plan: to pleasure dive part of the reef nearer to our present sheltered position.

Just as we were about to set off leaving Phil and Madge to recover from the adventure over a leisurely breakfast we heard, before we saw, the arrival of a pump-boat. It wasn't the engine we heard first but a voice over a megaphone. Suddenly it dawned on us that it was part of an election campaign and the electioneers appeared to be approaching a small settlement in the bay. This was even more remarkable than the poster in El Nido. Whatever their motives – whether they were canvassing or collecting votes for the impending election – the amount of time and energy made to reach the tiny, remote settlement of illiterate fishermen and their families was impressive. The boat pulled into the cove and we loaded the dinghy with our diving paraphernalia and set off with David as our ferryman and dive marshal, accompanied by Anna.

We stopped over the reef, in about three metres of water and a few metres from the vertical edge, to get into our diving gear. I had been given the task of anchoring the dinghy to coral. My mission was to find a secure rock of the right shape to tie up to. This wasn't a problem but sea-urchins and stone-fish – armed with toxic spines – were. If untreated the venom from stone-fish can be fatal. The other grave disadvantage of stone-fish, implied by their name, is the nature of their disguise. The Latin name: *synanceia horrida* – is especially pertinent. Success at hiding in whatever habitat they are living in is achieved by their camouflage: aided by a drab brownish colour with grey mottling, rough craggy heads and bodies form a perfect match to their surroundings and make it essential to scrutinise any surface one is likely to touch.

On one occasion, in Singapore, my daughter, Fiona, stepped off her wind-surfing board, in shallow sea, onto what was later believed to be a stone fish. At first she thought she had trodden on broken glass. She experienced searing pain and what appeared to be a fine gash, across the sole of her foot, was bleeding. In a matter of seconds her foot became swollen and the pain increased so intently that staff at the wind-surfing club telephoned for an ambulance. She was treated with anti-venom injections and pain killers at the hospital before being sent home.

By evening she was feverish and in such agony that I telephoned the hospital to re-admit her. The earlier treatment was repeated and her foot encased in ice. Back home as soon as the ice melted the agony returned. I encased her foot in a plastic bag of fresh ice-cubes and wrapped it in a towel. The ice acted as an anaesthetic – as soon as it melted the pain returned. After twenty-four hours we were able to let her foot thaw out but she couldn't walk on it for days. Since diving on abandoned oil rigs in Brunei I had learnt to recognise and avoid stone-fish. They hide on the bracings of the rigs and can be identified by the movements of their rather bulbous eyes and the just detectable fluttering of camouflaged fins.

The long black spines of the sea urchin make it easier to detect against a background of coral. Nevertheless, the effects of poison emitted from touching the brittle spines can be just as painful. I can vouch from personal experience that the Malaysian remedy I received, from a local boatman, after treading on a sea urchin – hammering the injected spines with a piece of wood to break them up, followed by applications of fresh lime – does ameliorate the pain; this treatment, repeated at intervals, ensured a relatively speedy recovery.

Now I was under the dinghy, hovering just above the surface of the coral alive with sea-urchins searching for a rock to use as an anchor. The urchins looked like the autumnal droppings of a plagued chestnut tree. I held onto a projection of rock just avoiding the tail end of a stone-fish. Since my only protection was the sting-suit I was wearing I was concerned that my floating limbs, waving in the current, might inadvertently brush an urchin's spines which could easily penetrate the lightweight material. Then to my right I saw an undercut boulder. I looped the rope below the bulge and tried to remember Tim's instructions for tying a bowline: 'Overlap the long end to form a circle (pond) – take the short end, push it up out of the pond and round the back of the long end (tree), in the pond again and pull.' With half my mind on venomous sea-creatures and the other focused on remembering instructions I couldn't be sure that I had succeeded in tying a bowline correctly. However, it looked secure and felt secure when I tugged. It would have to suffice.

Tim had decided to use a surface marker buoy, rather like taking a balloon for a walk. This would make it easier for David and Anna to see exactly where we were along the reef-face. We stepped over the edge and began our slow descent. As we dropped there were obvious changes in coral and plant-life – the reverse of vegetation changes a mountaineer might see as he ascends towards the peak but on a much smaller scale. In both instances the areas immediately above and below water-level are subject to erosion, especially forces of moving water, resulting in scanty vegetation. Beyond these regions warm temperatures and plenty of light foster bands of luxuriant and colourful growth. Higher and deeper as light and warmth decrease there is less diversity but plants and corals increase in size. Trees on forested mountain slopes grow taller in attempts to reach light while corals develop wide plate-like surfaces to catch as much of the light filtering down as possible. Finally, as temperatures drop towards mountain summits and in the depths of the sea where light and warmth can no longer penetrate, obvious growth thins and diminishes.

For the first few metres of our descent we were buffeted by the movement of waves and dropping past a rough dark wall. Then we were face to face with a sudden profusion of soft corals and sea fans which blossomed from the reef. Soft pinks and mauves dominated – their colours changing from deep blushing shades to pale subtle tones as they swayed in the still detectable movement of currents. A yellow feather-star gathered its long arms into a balletic pose as I brushed against it. A lime-green coral's long delicate fingers swayed as gracefully as the feathery fronds of a casuarina in a breeze. Equally colourful and varied fish hung like mobiles or darted among waving fronds.

After ten metres soft corals gave way to huge filigree fans and magnificent heads of antlers with luminescent mauve and purple tips as if the gardeners from 'Alice' had been let loose with pots of paint. A rainbow coloured wrasse darted into a crevice; an angel fish came face to face, boldly outstaring me. Below twenty metres the water was noticeably colder and the vertical reef edge sloped gently towards the sandy floor. The loose sand was easily stirred into a whirling fog. Tiny turquoise fish, the size of thumb-nails, popped in and out of the hollow fingers of an organ-pipe sponge; tube worms resembling honeysuckle flowers glowed and retracted petal-limbs as I stroked them. The head of a surprised moray eel popped out of an encrusted pipe as we passed.

I bumped into Tim as he was pausing to give the thumbs up sign. We surfaced and finned to the waiting dingy.

*****

The next stage of our journey to Coron Island was through Temple Passage, between a chain of islands. In the distance the north-west coast of the island presented an imposing vertical cliff-face some seven miles long and reaching to over 1,590 feet. It was evening by the time we neared the island. Tim was hoping for enough daylight to find our way into a volcanic fjord where he intended to anchor. As the sun dropped behind us a sliver of moon, in rosy sky, hung like a pendant over magnificent black clouds which grew into the shape of a dragon. The sky deepened to burnt sienna. Darkness fell like a curtain.

The rock face was now an awesome black edifice and we had the seemingly impossible task of finding a solitary mushroom rock which marked the narrow entry into the fjord. Tim was using a combination of piloting and natural features to navigate by and was on a heading of 160 degrees with the lights from Coron fishing wharf on a reciprocal bearing behind us. While there was still some daylight he had been able to focus on a dip in the skyline above the gap we were looking for but now, close up, we were facing a black wall. We were so close to the cliffs that he deemed it necessary to arm David and Anna with torches, and send them ahead in the dinghy. Meanwhile Phil and I stood on the bows shining our torches onto the rock face.

The gods must have been on our side for, directed by David's torchlight and echoing voice, the light from our torches picked out the mushroom rock and we followed the bouncing dinghy through the gap and into a narrow channel between reefs of coral into a black hole in the mountain. We dropped anchor in eighteen metres of water and the intrepid David set off in the dinghy to tie the stern to the nearest rock face to secure our position. Engine off we found ourselves suspended in a mighty silence. Across the fjord a fire was smouldering on the water's edge; the sound of a child crying rang into the night; a dog barked then the velvet silence returned. We were surrounded by black walls 100 metres high and above them a pool of sky crazy with stars.

Day 10

Not for the first time Madge's washing routine provided the early morning call. I forced myself to be reasonable by telling myself that everyone was different; it was the coolest part of the day and the best time to be active; it was just that we had different priorities. Tim looked like a beached whale. Not even the Titans doing their washing would rouse him this morning. I got up, put the kettle on to boil, and went on deck.

We were anchored to one side of the central circular section of the fjord, approximately 100 metres in diameter. To our stern was the hidden, narrow channel from Coron Bay through which we had sailed last night and at the opposite end, from a stony beach, a track led up the hillside. To the right there seemed to be another channel into the bay. Straight across from us, on our portside, a local family had set up home on a series of steps cut into the sloping scree. A thatched roof over an open-sided shack stood on one side of the stony beach while at the other end a two-tiered flimsy structure straggled up a slope roughly levelled into terraces. The remains of last night's fire were still smouldering; children and dogs played by the water's edge where two boats were moored.

In daylight the craggy rock walls took on the sculptured outlines of rows of conifers. Some of these, separated from the wall and standing on stone pedestals where the rock had been undercut, reached to over ten metres. Other sections, riddled with cracks and fissures, formed weird tortuous shapes as if strange creatures had been caught in the flow of hot lava and solidified. Straggly trees and shrubs grew from hollows or wherever they could get tenuous hold in patches of scree or behind sliding boulders. Near the water the rock had been eaten away and was riddled with a labyrinth of inlets and caverns leading into the heart of the mountain.

Considering that our surroundings could be seen as threatening, the ambience was magical and remarkable. We were hemmed in by precipitous bare rock walls interspersed by ragged patches of scree from falls of rock: all the symptoms of bad *chi*. However, we were anchored with the prow facing a hill-slope covered in grass and trees.

The stony track leading uphill looked as if it could be the bed of a stream during the wet season but now marked the passage of an underground river. We were surrounded by bad *chi* but aligned with good *chi* – even a dragon-line. It felt good – perhaps this accounted for our safe entry last night.

When everyone had assembled on deck Tim pointed to the opposite end of the fjord where, from the beach, a trail led up the hillside.

'If you follow that pathway to the top of the hill you'll have a magnificent view of the fjord and across Coron Bay. Over the hill the path leads down to a fresh inland lake. Well worth exploring,' he enthused. 'Take shampoo and towels. The water's soft. Excellent for washing. Even better for swimming.'

Madge, Phil, David and Anna made plans to set off immediately after breakfast, while Tim and I decided to explore later, in the cool of early evening. Breakfast over Tim acted as ferryman delivering the others to the beach for the start of the climb. As he returned and drew alongside, the engine putted to a halt restoring the tangible silence. His priority was to sort out charts and attend to minor repairs. While he was pre-occupied I found my dog-eared copy of *Foucault's Pendulum* and settled in the shade of the main sail to enjoy the luxury of space and quiet on deck and the first stirring of a breeze as cool air, rolling down the mountain slope, was pulled towards the solar-heated water of the bay.

I was roused from Eco's philosophising by the sound of paddles pulling against the water. A boy from the encampment across the fjord was passing in front of the *Star* making for a hidden outlet. As he paddled he sang in a voice as clear and pure as an angel's. Amplified by the natural acoustics of the place his untrained notes could have done justice to an operatic performance at any one of a range of notable venues. Here, a flotilla of yachts would be needed to house an opera company and audience. I felt privileged to be the

142

solitary audience at a brief but truly remarkable solo performance. As the boy's boat and voice were eclipsed by the wall of rock, a pump boat, laden with divers and diving equipment entered the fjord from our stern. Alerted by the throbbing engine Tim's head appeared through the hatch.

'Looks promising. Could well be a compressor on board. Air for us and possibly extra diving gear for David and Anna.'

The boat chugged towards the beach. We watched the divers unload their equipment and struggle up the slope with their tanks and gear – apparently intent on diving in the fresh water lake. There was still someone on board so we decided to take our cylinders over in the dinghy. We were in luck. The dive boat was from Coron town on Busuanga Island across the bay. There was just one problem. We were short of cash. In the end Tim traded his passport and arranged to retrieve it the next day when we exchanged travellers' cheques for cash in the bank at Coron. I could think of no other person with sufficient trust, or lack of caution, who would be willing to hand his passport to a stranger, in the middle of a fjord in the Philippines, for a dive. The transaction decided upon we arranged to return in an hour to collect our filled bottles and extra equipment for the other two divers. Until then we had the time to ourselves in one of the most romantic settings in the world.

By the time the crew returned from their fresh water jaunt the filled cylinders were ready and waiting. David and Anna had decided on a shallow dive in the fjord so leaving them to kit up, and Phil and Madge relaxing on deck, we set off finning our way backwards towards the channel and the reef edge. The drop, of some twenty-five metres, was to a sandy bottom covered in a bed of huge sculptured plants with curled beige leaves as delicate and brittle as brandy snaps. A few metres higher the reef-face was full of crevices from which overhanging plants, with drooping tendrils, created picturesque hiding places for hesitant fish. The most startling coral was, once again, in the shape of antlers with purple and luminous white tips – as if covered in hoar frost. Soft corals in brilliant purples, reds and orange grew between great white branches of lunar trees. Bright yellow and black banner fish hung between the limbs as if suspended on invisible strings. The colour, the silence, the overriding sense of a magical, lost world was pure magic.

At six metres, over a platform of coral, it was like looking down on a splendid and carefully tended rock garden. Irregular boulders decorated with antler heads of wintry bushes in white or yellow; whirling petals, filigree fans and pin-cushion corals – like legless mushrooms – ranging in size from a couple of inches across to the width of dinner plates. Exquisite, brightly coloured fish slipped and dozed between splashes of red and purple soft corals. Among waving fronds of lime green and blues a bright yellow and purple puff-ball flicked its tail as it swam away. A shoal of silver fish turned in unison, catching the light like tin-foil.

The mysterious combination of stillness and sudden movement in this crystalline world was unreal; eyes and fins moved rapidly and nervously. Movement, when it came, was sudden and darting; the movements of hunter and hunted: each, constantly on the look-out for food or predators. Smaller fish remained in the vicinity of fissures or cavities where they could rapidly disappear if threatened – a necessity since large predators arrived like torpedoes – quite literally out of the blue. I was haunted by vacant staring eyes and drooping mouths. It was as if a terrible sadness sprang from some primordial knowledge that aeons ago, when their ancestors developed lungs and limbs and invaded the land, they were left behind, trapped in their beautiful underworld.

As the sun fell behind the rock-wall Tim and I set off to find the freshwater lake. Leaving the dinghy tied to a rock at the foot of the slope, leading to the watershed between the fjord and the lake, we followed a trail between loose boulders, stained brown from underlying sedimentary rock. The 200 metres climb was steep. I could feel my heart knocking against my ribs with the exertion. At the top of the ridge there was a spectacular view of the fjord – the sheer dark sides cupping striped emerald and turquoise water and dwarfing the *Star of Siam* to a toy. Beyond the fjord the water of Coron Bay sparkled in late sunlight and distant mountains unfolded against blue sky.

On the other side the hill fell away to the freshwater lake, caught between its own towering craggy sides. The path down was less steep and there were more trees and scrubby grass. Once again, in addition to the grandeur, the most remarkable feature was the silence – like that of an ancient cathedral where every whisper is magnified and almost irreligious. There was an uncanny feeling of hidden life and watching eyes. An avalanche of massive boulders, stained red-brown, marked the beginning of the lake. It was about 100 metres across and stretched before us for some 300 metres in length. At the far end the sides fell away and the water extended to left and right forming the horizontal bar of a T.

Stripping down to swimming gear, we left our clothes and cameras in a hollow at the water's edge then gingerly picked our way over the slimy and stony bottom towards a fallen tree lying in several feet of brackish water. The trunk provided a support and places to lodge bottles of shampoo and towels. The water had the texture of milk and we were soon covered in a froth of bubbles. Without speaking we started swimming losing our bubbles in widening concentric rings which fanned out until they reached the undercut sides of rock. Now the only sound was the slapping of our waves into unseen tunnels and crevices. In the deep darkness of the water I sensed an increasing and mighty depth beneath me and the presence of some prehistoric creature watching white limbs sliding over its head.

When we reached the far end of the lake we turned into the left-hand branch of the bar, open to the last evanescent shafts of sunlight. We were heading for a stony cove but it was difficult and uncomfortable to stand and there was nowhere to sit or explore. It was also growing dark and our clothes and cameras, left at the far end, were now out of sight. I was becoming increasingly uneasy about watching eyes. I had heard tales about primitive tribes, living in the folds of hills. It is believed that their ancestors, known by the Spaniards as *Guambianos*, had a reputation for the same ferocity as the sea-pirates, killing all upon whom they could lay their hands.

As darkness grew the mysterious nature of the place increased. Over and above the slapping of water under the cliffs there were now sudden bursts of noise, scuffles and night cries. By the time we emerged the last of daylight was fading. Thankful to find our clothes and belongings where we had left them we dressed and feeling more self-possessed picked our way uphill to the ridge. The *Star's* riding light was a beacon and guide to our downhill pathway and across the dark water.

Day 11

The next morning we left our secret fjord and sailed across the bay to Coron Town on Busuanga Island. We were in need of fresh-water, fruit, vegetables, bread, more ice, air for our cylinders as well as cash to be exchanged for Tim's passport. We arrived to find several yachts at anchor in the bay and rows of local streamlined boats with high curved prows, resembling Viking warships, ready for action.

Before we had time to tie the dinghy to a metal ring in the harbour wall we were faced by a row of waiting taxis – motor-cycles with attached side-cars: the only mode of transport to reach the town – ten minutes ride away on the other side of the bay. Three was the optimum number of passengers so we split into two groups. I opted to ride pillion while my fellow travellers, Phil and Tim, squeezed into the side-car – the dive cylinders looking grotesquely phallic between their knees. With the others in tow, we set off, along the National Highway – a narrow tarmac road full of pot-holes. I soon learnt the hazards of riding pillion. Apart from the danger of bouncing off as we careered over pot-holes my knees were an extra hazard – yet another disadvantage of long legs. I had to sit side-saddle and balance one foot on top of the other on the metal foot-support, press my knees against the side of the bike to prevent knee-amputation by oncoming traffic and hang on to the driver for fear of shooting off the back.

On the coast side of the highway ramshackle stilt houses waded along the water's edge and climbed up the banks, leaning drunkenly against each other for tenuous support. Inland the houses were larger, separate and surrounded by trees. We passed an impressive avenue leading to the College of Fishing and a large sign to Ford's Driving Centre. This was civilisation indeed. Sections of the road were lined with frangipani and trees heavy with pink blossom – a tropical version of an English avenue in spring.

The dive centre was located on the water-front among a collection of stilt-houses, linked by rotting walkways and straggling over curry-coloured water. Leaving the others to explore I assisted Tim, carrying the cylinders over the creaking walkways to a central area surrounded by potted plants. The place seemed to be locked and, apart from a few curious locals who were on our trail, was deserted. Eventually, Tim made one of them understand that we wanted the owner. He disappeared and returned a few minutes later followed by a plump, sarong-clad, woman claiming to be the owner's wife. We explained about the passport. She looked blank and said she didn't know. We must see her husband. His office was locked.

'When?' Tim asked. 'What time?' he added, pointing to his watch.

'Lunch-time,' she said. 'Maybe, lunch-time. He take divers.'

'Wonderful! Could be all day,' I muttered. 'Could be a week if it's a wreck.'

More pragmatic and more trusting Tim explained to the woman that we were going to get cash from the bank for her husband, who had his passport.

'He must give me my passport. You tell him. We'll come back at one o'clock. We'll leave our cylinders,' he added. 'We need air. We'll collect them at one o'clock too.'

Built in a quadrangle, the town boasted a bank, a selection of general stores and a market. The heat, wide dusty streets and wooden buildings reminded me of the Mid-West. I expected to hear the clatter of hooves, gun shots and to see John Wayne swaggering round a corner at any moment. However, the only sound was that of a pig screeching from the slaughterhouse on the waterfront. We passed a general store where Tim purchased two rubber balls.

'It's a secret,' he said, enjoying my puzzled expression. 'I'll reveal all back on the Star – and no facetious comments either,' he added in anticipation.

I left him hugging the balls and his secret while we went in search of the bank. We walked up the first side of the quadrangle before we realised we had gone straight past it. Hardly surprising since its frontage was no more imposing than that of surrounding shops and stores. Inside it consisted of one room with three desks. Behind each desk sat a smiling assistant. There were no other customers so our transactions were soon complete. We emerged to find Phil and Madge waiting on the doorstep.

'We've found a decent eating place and a bar. The others are already imbibing,' Phil explained.

We followed them through the edge of the market which straggled along the waterfront, between stalls of clothes, fruit, vegetables, and fish. Pigs and chickens, strung upside down by their legs, dripped blood and were surrounded by clouds of flies. At one side was an alley lined with bars where locals were hiding from the sun, drinking and playing cards. Phil was pointing to a flight of steps leading up the side of a partially completed building.

'Up here,' he said leading the way.

Belonging to an enterprising Dutchman, the unfinished project, comprising a two storey building with facilities for visitors – especially divers attracted by local reefs and Japanese wrecks from World War Two – was still underway. The restaurant was complete and overlooked the sparkling bay and the mountains of Coron Island. The entrance to the fjord was hidden in the folds of the rock-curtain fronting the island. In contrast, in the water below, stilt houses in various stages of collapse, waded in sludge-brown water that was used as a refuse tip and sewer by the town's people. The stench of sewage and rotting matter, partly held at bay by overhead fans, came in short bursts or, from time to time, mingled sickeningly with whiffs of garlic and chilli from the kitchen. A group of local businessmen hunched round a table were silently and systematically lifting food from plate to mouth with nimble extended chop-stick fingers. An attractive Filipino girl, who spoke commendable English, brought us beers and took our orders for prawns, vegetables and rice. After the meal Tim and Phil went to claim the passport and collect the cylinders while the rest of us went in search of taxis to take us to the harbour.

Once we were back on the *Star* Tim revealed the nature of his secret. He volunteered me to fit the rubber balls to the ends of the spreaders to protect the sails from rubbing and wearing; each had been split on one side by two crossed cuts. To do this I had to sit in the boatswain's chair – rather like a canvas nappy and attached to a rope by a metal shackle – and then be winched two-thirds of the way up the mast to the level of the spreaders.

'Trust me,' was Tim's reassurance. 'Trust me and trust the shackle. It can take ten times your weight.'

I tried to think of a good reason for trusting Tim or shackles. I couldn't. My first sailing experience in Brunei was learning to sail Hobie-Cats with Tim as my instructor when, in his words, I was no more than 'flexible ballast'. It was on a perfect Hobie-Cat sailing day: a steady wind and high waves until Tim, at the helm, decided to demonstrate his sailing and trapezing skills synonymously. The lesson ended disastrously when his trapeze line broke and he catapulted me and the Hobie-Cat into the deep. The greatest danger came from my bleeding arms, making me attractive bait for lurking sharks. Now with camera round my neck, rubber balls, sellotape and scissors in my lap, I put myself in the hands of fate as I was slowly hauled into the air. David was turning the winch and Tim tailing and monitoring progress. I held onto the rope and tucked my feet lightly round the mast, ready to cling like a monkey if something gave. I looked down watching Tim's body growing smaller and legless and the swaying deck further away and yet more solid. I imagined myself falling – splattered on the deck like a fledgling.

Taking photographs was an antidote to fear and a bird's eye view of the deck and boats in the bay was worth capturing. Once at the level of the spreaders I had to swing my way across to the outer tip. Now, without the solid mast for support, I was even more vulnerable, but I had a task to perform and once in position there was the slanting shroud to wrap my feet round which stopped me swinging perilously like the last pear of summer. Ball taped into place I then had to swing across to the opposite side and repeat the operation.

'You may as well go to the top now you're up there,' Tim yelled, signalling to David to keep winding.

I started to rise conscious of the strain of my weight on the rope pitted against David's muscles as he turned the winch. I kept my legs looped round the mast and let the rope slip through my hands. I wondered if I could remember the technique I had learnt in the gym at school of climbing down a pole or rope, or if I would slither down helter-skelter, the rope tearing and burning my flesh, and land with a resounding crash. Tim's upturned face looked like a bearded moon. His body and legs had all but disappeared. Suddenly I was there, level with the top of the mast and as unstable as a hornbill perched at the top of a swaying casuarina. Holding on with my left hand I manoeuvred my camera into position and took several shots of the deck and some more of miniature boats in the bay. Then I gave a 'thumbs up' sign to the watching crew.

'Ok.' Tim yelled, 'Mission accomplished. We're bringing you down.'

A week after we returned from the cruise Tim handed me a surprise.

'A memento,' he said offering me a broken shackle.

'Not the one,' I faltered, fingering the broken pin. 'Not the one you told me to trust?'

'The very one,' he replied. 'But not to worry. It gave on the No 2 Jib – in high winds – much heavier, much more strain than you.'

By the time I was safely on deck there was quite a party going on. We had been joined by the Dutch skipper of a schooner and Peter, an ageing Filipino – both of whom knew Tim and the *Star* from previous trips. Peter looked especially delighted to be on board and drinking warm beer with us – his dark eyes disappearing into leathery folds of skin every time he smiled. Then our socialising was disrupted by the arrival of Phil; acting as ferryman he was bringing us supplies of ice. We formed a human chain from dinghy to galley to transfer slippery blocks – the size of thick paving slabs – to the ice-box. Just as we finished, a yacht, flying the Canadian flag, drew up to within hailing distance. Once the crew had established that the tide level was safe for twenty-four hours they dropped anchor. Unfortunately, it was time for us to lift our anchor and leave. As we made final preparations for departure I caught a glimpse of Peter's hunched frame paddling towards the jetty; the missing outrigger on the port side of his boat causing it to heel like a maimed crab.

The sun was setting as we left Coron Bay to begin the homeward leg of our journey. The plan was to sail south, parallel to the eastern coast of Palawan to Honda Bay. From there it was a few hours sailing to Puerto Princesa where we had arranged to leave the *Star of Siam* for the next crew from Brunei. They would fly in from Manila as we were flying out. Madge, especially, was relaxed and excited at the thought of bars, shops and hotel facilities in Manila.

Day 12

It was our turn to do the dreaded Middle-watch and, once again, we had to be especially vigilant for rocks and islands. Predictably wind and sea grew turbulent during the longest, darkest hours. Madge woke twice from nightmares to tell us we had run aground. For me it was more like re-entering the living nightmare of nights on the first part of the trip. Hunched in my yellow waterproof I clung onto the wheel. The *Star* was under constant attack from rolling foam-crested hills. No sooner had one collapsed and floundered across the deck than another followed. We lunged into each rearing wave and rolled to port as it broke, sails straining. I was battling to keep her on a constant heading. I could see Tim's head and shoulders bent over the chart table. With aching arms and cramp in the foot that was pressed against the adjacent port bench, to keep me balanced, I was convinced that four a.m. would never come.

By mid-morning there was so little wind that we seemed to be rocking on the spot. We needed to conserve diesel so sails were up and engine off. The mainsail was flogging in and out with almighty gunshot cracks. Progress was so slow that Tim decided it was safe to have bath-time on the move. We went through the now familiar routine but without enthusiasm. The novelty had worn off. As day progressed the heat increased: sweltering below deck – merciless above. With the sun overhead there was little shelter. Finally, Tim conceded that the wind wasn't going to pick up as expected. We took down the jib, reefed the mainsail and handed the controls to George. The constant throb of the engine was comforting compared to the spasmodic flogging of the sail and, at least, it felt as if we were going somewhere. I was feeling unsociable and started behaving like a mole. By standing on the berth in our cabin and placing my hands either side of the hatch I could jump and hoist myself up using the hatch as a doorway, avoiding the galley steps and cockpit. Making myself a nest among the folds of the jib at the tip of the prow I curled up with Umberto Eco.

The rest of the crew were generally apathetic or unwell. David and Anna were expending the greatest amount of energy on scrabble; Phil and Madge alternately reading and lazing. Even Tim was slumped in a heap in the cabin. It could have been the food we had eaten at Coron Bay or it could be general inertia from the heat, lack of forward motion and the endless, restless empty vista of sea. I began to feel like a character in Sartre's *No Exit*. Day drifted into evening. I had been exercising great control by waiting until six a.m.

before imbibing in the last G and T. When the magic hour arrived I couldn't find the tonic. It was buried under the huge slabs of ice we had picked up yesterday. Then Phil surprised us all by unveiling hidden domestic prowess. He cooked a palatable evening meal of *chilli con carne* and pasta.

Day 13

The sun rose behind us and grey mountains unfolded ahead as we approached Honda Bay. The mountains, forming the dip-slope of the precipitous north-west facing cliffs we were now so familiar with, were more widely spread and softer in outline. On the other hand the bay was treacherous with reefs, lagoons, estuaries, mangrove islands and rocks, awash at low tide requiring all of our navigating expertise. We were on the opposite side of Palawan to Jock Gordon's Place and looking for a reciprocal guest-house on Meara Island, built and run by Franz, an enterprising Austrian. On the chart the island looked like a flying fish. Now, close up we were sailing parallel to the mangrove swamps which constituted the tail. We rounded the curve of the fin and there in a white cove surrounded by palm trees was a remarkable roundhouse with a beehive thatched roof.

Once the Star was anchored we set off in the dingy towards a somewhat rickety jetty to be met and welcomed by Franz. Short and stocky with a Father Christmas grey beard and pale blue eyes he guided us to his island home where, he explained, he had been established for seven years. His house had two advantages over Jock's Place which ensured a steady trickle of visitors: accessibility and facilities for divers. Puerto Princesa, with its airport, could be reached in a couple of hours by pump-boat and he had a compressor for filling dive cylinders, equipment for hire and a boy to ferry divers to the best local reefs. A naval architect by trade he continued to draw and build boats in his present life. His thirty eight foot yacht, anchored in front of the house, was one of his accomplishments – the design of a new boat was on a drawing-board in the lounge. During our brief stay a large package was delivered. It turned out to be a do-it-yourself kit for a microlight aircraft. Franz was taking to the sky.

Franz was also a warm and genial host and his open plan roundhouse comfortable and relaxing. In addition to the traditional cane furniture inside, woven hammocks strung from coconut trees tempted idleness in the garden. I was drifting towards sleep in one when Franz, pointing to a cluster of coconuts over my head, advised me to change ends. It was then I remembered reading in the SAS Survival Manual that there were more deaths from falling coconuts than from snake-bites in Asia. It would be an ignominious end but a wonderful place to be buried. During the afternoon Franz set off by pump-boat for Puerto Princesa to order supplies of diesel and fresh water, leaving one of his staff to take us out to a reef.

The plan was to end the day with a night-dive. Everything pointed to abandoning the plan: Tim and I had been up since four a.m. and had enjoyed an afternoon reef-dive. By the time we finished the evening meal it was after nine p.m.; the tide was now far out and we had to move our dive cylinders and gear from the stranded dinghy to the end of the 200 meter wooden-slatted jetty by moonlight. We ignored all warning signs.

The first task was to rescue the equipment. We had left the dinghy moored halfway along the jetty, next to a set of steps, but the tide had retreated to the far end, just a few metres from a reef-edge. There was a half-moon and enough light to see what we were doing. Tim waded through the brackish water, threaded with mangrove grass and the roots of trees and, no doubt, home to a multitude of slimy poisonous creatures. When he reached the dinghy he passed each item up the steps to me. Next we made several journeys carrying them to the end of the jetty while trying not to fall through or trip on uneven slats. Fortunately, there was a pump-boat moored to the steps at the end so we lifted all the gear down into the boat and began the final stages of preparation.

The boat turned out to be a small and unstable base and it was dark in the shadow of the jetty so kitting up was more by feel than sight. I gazed across the huge expanse of dark slack sea. Wave movement was barely visible or audible. Behind us the lights of the house looked inviting. Then Tim discovered that his underwater torch wasn't working. We had one light between us – enough to attract but not see sharks. Tim took the remaining torch. I waited for him to tumble backwards and give the ok sign then followed. We swam a few metres to the reef edge; Tim gave the thumbs down sign and we began our slow descent into the night-black hole of the Sulu Sea with nothing but the dancing beam of the torch, on the wall of coral, to keep us company.

I had not expected it to be so dark. The moon was behind the reef-wall and ineffectual. Tim took my hand and switched off the torch. I could see nothing and hear only my laboured umbilical breathing. I was at once in a narrow black tunnel and an immense underwater vacuum. We had decided to stay at fifteen metres, swim along the reef-wall, timing our progress and noting any distinctive features before turning back along the same route. I followed the torch's beam darting and stopping along the wall. Bright red and orange corals were covered in furry glowing polyps. Fish, too, glowed in reds, pinks and orange as if under x-ray or suffused by the colour of blood. Sleeping open-eyed fish hung motionless or shot away into darkness.

I knew that fish were attracted to light and that those who live in the permanent realms of darkness in the depths of the ocean create their own, communicating through luminescent or phosphorescent winks and flashes. One of the most fascinating specimens, the deep-sea angler fish, sports a glowing green globe which it can droop in front of its mouth. This devious device is dangled, like a Christmas tree bulb to attract prey. When an inquisitive fish approaches to investigate, the angler opens its cavernous jaws and swallows its victim. There were no lights winking or flashing round us. Whatever was there, watching our light, was as dark, silent and undetectable as our surroundings.

I recalled the tale of a diving companion in Brunei, that large fish, attracted by light, become curious – and how on a night-dive, a huge fish following his torch-light had swum between him and the hose to his regulator, dragging it from his mouth. In a state of momentary panic, thinking his air-line had been severed, he swam to his buddy signalling his need for air. In the dark his buddy didn't understand. Desperate he pulled at his Octopus Rig. At this, his buddy knew there was a problem and they both ascended. It wasn't until they surfaced they realised that, although the hose had been wrenched from his mouth, it was still intact.

I tried looking over my shoulder, to left, to right, ahead. Nothing. We were blind except for the solitary dancing beam from the torch. I began to find following the light tiring. The person holding and controlling the light is synchronised: hand, brain, eye – but attempting to follow someone else's irregular movement required absolute concentration. I was trying to anticipate the direction. I wanted it to remain still. I became disorientated and started bumping into lumps of coral, knocking against the reef wall, dragging my legs over unseen surfaces, swimming into sticky fronds. I was no longer interested in fish or coral but conscious only of my breathing. My mouth tasted of iron. My instinct was to pull out the regulator and breathe fresh air. Just then Tim stopped and using the torch on his hands, signalled our return. At first I felt relief then I wanted to surface but reasoned with myself. He would think it was an emergency. Was it an emergency? It would be a long and arduous surface swim to the boat, perhaps against the tide. I signalled ok and Tim turned to begin the swim back.

I stayed close to him, following his waving fins like a well-trained dog – stopping when he stopped. Focusing on the light was too tiring; the sense of being in a narrow tunnel – of thick darkness – increased. Even our horizontal positions and finning suggested movement through a tunnel. The restless beam of light explored the wall. I followed it as a directive but without observing, like an exhausted child being led through a museum. My mouth and throat were dry, my breathing asthmatic. I made a conscious effort to breathe slowly and to move with slow regular finning strokes. I knew that Tim was as aware of my presence behind him as I was of the shapeless form ahead of me. We had our own dragon-line. Then, somehow, I found I was above him bumping against the reef-wall. I looked down into the searchlight, dumped air, dropped and settled into a wobbly buoyancy.

Tim stopped. I bumped into him. He signalled ascent. We faced each other holding hands. I resisted the temptation to fin. Nevertheless, I was overtaking him, pulling him with me. We burst through the sea's skin into moonlight just a few metres from the pump-boat.

Day 14

The following morning Franz was waiting to tell us that there was an air-traffic controllers' strike in Manila and that Royal Brunei, among other airlines, had cancelled all flights. Further news on the radio revealed there was also a pre-election electricity strike and from what we knew about Manila gun-fighting in the streets would not be unusual. Manila was no longer an attractive or practical proposition and it was unlikely we would be able to fly there from Puerto

Princesa as planned. We faced two major problems: everyone had to return to work in three days time and we had arranged to leave the *Star* in Puerto Princesa for the next crew. If we sailed to Puerto Princesa we would be stranded and the next crew would not be able to fly in.

We had no choice but to sail the *Star of Siam* to Kota Kinabalu in Sabah. It was more likely that we would be able to fly out from there. We left Tim on the telephone to Brunei sorting out our delayed return and air-tickets. Nobody, except Tim, looked happy about the prospect of another three to four days and nights sailing. Madge, especially, was crestfallen.

We left Meara island in early afternoon after surviving near disaster; Phil spotted that the men delivering drinking water and fuel were about to pour water into the fuel tank. Fortunately, his timely detection prevented real damage.

*****

Night watch: wind and sea were unusually calm so we put George in charge and took turns to sleep and helm. Tim was asleep. I was sitting behind the wheel in a state of semi-trance, mesmerised by the brilliance of the stars, the vastness of the sky. The shoulders of the sky appeared translucent as if the skin had been overstretched like a balloon that has been blown up too high. Overhead and at the water's edge it was deep blue. Suddenly I was intensely aware of my own insignificance juxtaposed against my own particular importance. Alone and diminutive in this immense night-blue world of ocean and sky it wasn't difficult to believe in an overwhelming and eternal presence. When I looked at the stars my eyes were invariably drawn to the Southern Cross. It was the constellation I would always remember – the most startling and thought provoking. That morning

I'd come across the following passage in Umberto Eco's *Foucault's Pendulum:*

When the Argonauts find the Golden Fleece their ship is borne into the Milky Way, in the astral sky, where the luminous nature of God is made manifest by the Southern Cross, the Triangle and the Altar. The Triangle symbolises the Holy Trinity, the Cross the divine Sacrifice of love, and the Altar is the table of the Supper, on which stood the cup of the Resurrection ...

Above me the Milky Way was strewn across the sky like a discarded diamond-studded wedding veil. Then Satnav's alarm roused me from my philosophising. Tim looked like the sleeping dead. I went below relieved to find the chart table as near to horizontal as it had ever been. Estimated Position: 120. 5E/ 10 N. I measured and pencilled in the two lines fixing them where they crossed with a small circle – a star of sorts. I wrote 10.45 p.m. alongside the fix. But even as I marked it time and our position had changed. I ran my finger over all the other stars marked on the chart, tracing our journey along the west coast of Palawan, through Dicabaito Channel and Temple Passage into the Sulu Sea and our magic fjord – across Coron Bay to Busuanga Island and down the east coast of Palawan to Honda Bay. How familiar and evocative all the names were now. A shadow fell over me and the table.

'How are we doing?' Tim asked, leaning over me to examine the chart. 'Ok', he continued in answer to my yawn. 'You collapse. I'll make tea.'

Day 15

We were woken by sounds of excitement on deck. Dolphins and flying fish. The dolphins were either asleep or lazing – the tips of their fins protruding above the surface like pieces of floating buttress roots. By contrast the fish were electric and flying in all directions. A band of cloud edged overhead of us depositing the first rain-shower of the trip but, unfortunately, not enough to salvage. Tim served toast and honey for breakfast. We sat cross-legged in our cabin, munching and licking sticky fingers like a couple of kids on a camping trip. After breakfast I became unusually domestic washing out my rotting sarongs and Tim's stiff T-shirts when I became aware of what I can only describe as a presence. I looked down to see the bows of the ship were surrounded by dolphins – swooping, dipping, rising in perfect rhythmic patterns, sometimes singly, sometimes in pairs or triplets.

'Dolphins!' I called. 'Dolphins. Quick. Come quickly!'

Within seconds we were all clustered round the prow, cameras whirring and clicking, as landlocked and clumsy as they were graceful and free.

It seemed as if they were playing a game with us – amusing themselves rather than amusing us and as if they were aware of our limitations and their superiority but without condescension. They moved with the rhythm and speed of the waves churned by the prow. They were part of the waves, rising with them and then springing over them in fluid curves before plunging back and across the front of the prow, exchanging sides with perfect timing and synchronisation. They never quite left the water. As their heads lifted, dipped and re-entered so their tails followed turning with the curve of the wave. Their silver silhouettes streamed beneath and

161

against the flow of water but keeping pace with us. Sometimes it was as if they were attached to the prow by reins, urging us to go faster, pulling us through the water effortlessly and untiringly until they were tired of the game. They stayed with us for an hour then slipped away, disappearing as inconspicuously as they had arrived. Pure magic.

We saw nothing else all day. Wind: nil. Sun: unremitting.

Day 16

Another night with no wind, calm sea and George in control. The moon looked like half an Edam cheese with a lightbulb inside. This was followed by a long, hot, windless day. Apart from half the cockpit, already inhabited by David, Anna and Phil, there was no shade on deck. Anna was crouched on the seat next to David shaving and grooming him. Phil was staring fixedly at the sea. From noon till three p.m. the still heat was so unbearable that I could neither read nor sleep. I sat as in a coma, beneath the hatch, dreaming of a breeze, rivulets of sweat trickling and dripping from me. The Ancient Mariner's, *'hot and copper sky'* and *'bloody sun at noon'* were all too real.

Later in the afternoon a few flying fish and a flock of birds that flashed white as they turned in unison were the only distractions. There was just enough gin left for a last sundowner. Fate must have prevented me from getting at the tonic previously. My need was much greater now.

Tim had been on the radio to Brunei for some time relaying and receiving messages about our unavoidable, delayed return to work; the cancelled air tickets from Puerto Princesa and Manila and the new tickets from Kota Kinabalu. He emerged with the cheering news that the Government Department I worked for in Brunei was: 'not pleased – repeat – not pleased' with my delay. This set my imagination racing about the sort of reception I would receive – at worst, I decided, or perhaps, at best I would be given my marching orders. The others were employed by Shell, who adopted a more reasonable attitude towards the vicissitudes of travel in this part of the world.

'The next piece of news,' Tim warned, 'affects us all. You may not like this,' he continued, 'but consider it and let me know. We can't be certain of flights from KK. This will mean further delays – but we can sail the Star back to Brunei. It will probably take another twenty-four hours. At least we'll be home and dry and so will the Star.'

There was a numb reaction at first then Madge exploded.

'I won't – I can't spend another night on this boat – not after tonight. I need a shower. I need clean clothes!'

Kevin paused. Everyone looked at him.

'We must consider everyone,' he explained. 'This crew – the Star – the next crew. The strike's caused problems – some people can't alter their dates for leave – they'll be short of qualified sailors.'

The rest of us were philosophical though once again no-one, except Tim, was keen on more sailing.

'I'd rather spend time in K.K.' David responded.

'There's no Club Med!' I teased.

'No, but there is the Tanjung Aru Hotel. Proper food – a swimming pool.'

'Yes,' added Madge glad of some support, 'and showers and shops.'

Anna was silent. Phil was his logical phlegmatic self, willing with me to support Tim if necessary but in the end the balance of opinion resulted in a decision to leave the *Star* in Kota Kinabalu. There would have been problems with immigration if the crew had split at this juncture.

In a matter of hours we would be sailing into the bay. We were a motley crew nevertheless we had bonded together and shared our skills, especially in times of need. It had been a cruise to remember. I closed my eyes. I could see Mount Kinabalu's shoulders emerging from a halo of cloud – planes taking off from the runway, streaking like bullets across the sky. Civilisation and the rest of the world were on the horizon.

Temple of the Tooth, Kandy, Sri Lanka

Elephant Ride – Mahaweli River, Kandy, Sri Lanka

New Oriental Hotel – Guest Room, Galle

Groot Kerk – Dutch Church, Galle (1755)

Suburbs of walled city of Galle

Lighthouse, within Galle Fort

Ancient Buddhist city, Anuradhapura

Monastery: Anuradhapura

Moonstone at monastery entrance, Anuradhapura

Guardstone: Abhayagiri Monastery

The Sage: Buddhist monk, Polonnaruwa

12th Century Buddhas cut from granite wall

Seated 12th Century Buddha

12th Century Buddhas, Dambulla Caves

Frescoes, Dambulla Caves

Yosuf, houseboat owner, Lake Nagin, Kashmir

Flower salesman, Lake Nagin

Family homes, Lake Nagin

Family houseboats, Srinagar

Men smoking hubbly bubblies, Srinagar

Wash day, Srinigar

Women carrying bundles of wood, Gulmarg

Buddhist Monks, Doi Suthep Temple, Chiang Mai

Doi Suthep Temple Bell

Golden umbrella & temple spire

Putting Gold Leaf on a statue of Buddha

Roadside craft stall – en route to Chiang Rai

Children from Lawa Hill Tribe selling beaded jewellery

Golden Triangle, countries separated by the Mekong River

Thailand's border with Burma, Mae Sai

Swissippini Cottage, Port Barton, Palawan

Filipino Man with fighting cock

Star of Siam anchored offshore, Port Barton

Elm Street Quarters, El Nido

Sunrise, Dicabaito Channel

Coral through gin clear water

View of coral from the deck

Village on water's edge, Dicabaito Island

Star of Siam anchored in volcanic fjord

Approaching Franz's Roundhouse, Meara Island

Author fixing split balls on the spreader

Skipper and deck from spreader

Sand mud walls of Ghadames, Libya

Dome and tower of mosque

Entrance to men's quarters

Decorated walls of women's quarters

Salt lakes: Hammadah al Hamra

Unspoilt dunes of the Fezzan

Elephants crossing Narayani River, Nepal

Unexpected encounter, Chitwan National Park

View to River Modi Khola

Village school perched on hillside, Kyumi

Annapurna from Kimche

Precariously positioned farms follow mountain ridge

Spire of Monkey Temple, Kathmandu

Baruk Beach, Tioman Island

View to Bushman Bar

Monitor Lizard, Baruk River Estuary

Mentawak waterfall

View from rain forest to South China Sea

Rain forest from Besar River

Evening light from Bushman Bar

Ali, dhow owner- cum-skipper, Musandam, Oman

Dolphin escorting dhow, Khor Ash Sham

Khasab Fort stands guard over old settlement

Mountain track to Rawdah Bowl

Ancient Shihuh settlement, Jebel Harim

Dhow petroglyph, Tawi

Horseman warrior petroglyph, Tawi

Khor Nadj Fjord in evening light

Clouds Hill, former home of Lawrence of Arabia, Dorset

The Lord is my light: stone book on Lawrence's grave

Entrance to Corfe Castle

Kingston Lacy: former home of Bankes family

Gold Hill, Shaftsbury

Tyneham Church with ghostly image of child on a swing

Coastal path, Whiteway Hill

13th Century Moorish Castle, Antequera, Spain

Competa straddling the hillside

Precariously balanced limestone pillars

Limestone formations Torcal Park

Narrow streets define the once impregnable city of Ronda

Richard contemplating summer snow in the Sierra Nevada

Cliffs of Moher, Galway, Ireland

Richard focused on Alcock and Brown memorial

Blennerville Windmill

Ned Natterjack's Bar, Castlegregory

Celtic Cross, Killiney Churchyard

Ancient beehive huts, Dingle Peninsula

South Pole Inn, Annascaul

Behind Libya's Closed Doors

1993. At this time – some five years after the Lockerbie bombing – although Gaddafi was still holding on to power there had been several attempts on his life and rumours of an attempted coup were rife. The country was under sanctions; the only 'foreigners' allowed into Libya were those employed in different sections of the oil industry – largely from Canada and the UK. My posting, as an English Language instructor, came with a range of unexpected restrictions: passports were taken on arrival and withheld until the annual leave; tourism didn't exist and independent travel was looked upon with deep suspicion. Nevertheless, such were the attractions of this isolated country – ranging from the remains of magnificent Roman cities fringing the coastline to unspoilt desert settlements deep in the Sahara that I was one, among a handful of resident expatriates who couldn't resist the temptation to explore. In spite of being arrested, interrogated at Central Intelligence and accused of working for the CIA, while en route to visit the Roman city of Leptis Magna, my enthusiasm had not been dampened.

In common with Brunei the way to escape the restrictions of daily life was through engaging in water sports. Boats, considered a means of escape, were forbidden. Diving was the alternative. The base for refilling diving cylinders was at Skanska – a private club – one of the few places in Libya with a bar where those currently 'in favour' met for a drink and to catch up on the latest news. A final visit to Skanska is captured in the poem, *Desert Rose* which also sets the scene for a exploring the ancient desert city of Ghadames.

Desert Rose

Released from the thrumming heart
of the Sahara, the Ghibli's[2] hot breath scours
pavements where dark men brewing tea crouch
and mutter. Rumours of the attempted coup

glow like hot coals. It is said, that Skanska,
the only oasis in this desert, had been raided.
Raped wine vats gape like cavities
from trees uprooted in a gale. The owner's

under house arrest. Her gun-running days
for Gaddafi erased. They say, her partner's
revolutionary ways have been paid for
in blood. Today, I slipped past the guard

into Skanska. Only the pregnant camel stirred.
She sifted through rotting fruit,
stared blankly. At my feet
a severed sheep's head buzzed with flies.

---

[2] *Ghibli:* hot desert wind

Sleek and alert as a desert rat

Gaddafi moves camp from day to day.

The media's strangled silence gurgles.

Still I write postcards as if you receive them.

Only a desert rose can survive this heat,

the abrasive murmuring wind.

They've had my passport for two months now.

I've heard the borders are closed.

Do it Yourself Tourism

After a brief interlude the tourist department had once again gone into hibernation. It was do-it-yourself tourism or nothing. Memories of being tailed by security, on a recent solo visit to the remains of the Roman city of Sabratha, had reinforced the need to find a like-minded companion to explore further afield as I planned. Then a timely invitation from Paula, an expat friend, to spend an evening at the Darts' Club arrived. This she assured me was the most likely place to meet someone as intent on travel as I was. Weekly meetings were held on a rotation basis at the houses of committee members and the next was to take place at a nearby oil company compound adjoining the beach.

'It has to be American,' I responded on learning the complex was named Friendship Village. 'Only Americans could christen a compound in Libya with such a name.'

'Originally, it was,' Paula confirmed steering me between rows of terraced sandstone villas with peeling paint, mould growing up the walls and shutters hanging from broken hinges. 'But believe it or not, it was quite upmarket in Esso days. It was once an American stronghold with a range of intercontinental restaurants and trendy shops in the main street while the beach was a hive of activity: water sports, cafes – the lot.'

Looking at the almost slum conditions of the compound and from my experiences of life in Libya so far, although I could understand some of the reasons for people being drawn to live and work here, I found it difficult to understand what kept them – sometimes for a working lifetime. As we walked Paula enlightened me about the 'Golden Handcuff Syndrome': the addictive stashing away of tax-free savings that takes hold so that one is never ready to leave.

'There's nothing to spend it on here so saving is easy,' she explained.

'Then there are those who become distanced from the real world – psychologically as well as physically. Many find it impossible to settle when they go back. John, our host for the evening and nearing retirement had lived here for decades. That's his house,' she said pointing to the end of a nearby terrace. 'I suspect Pete and I are of the same ilk. At first we couldn't wait to get out. Then without realising, it grew on us. Coming-up for ten years now. Saving for a retreat in the European sun. Security!' she warned, suddenly lowering her voice.

At that moment I saw the outline of a guard smoking and leaning against the only working and dimly lit lamp-post on the compound. The ubiquitous Kalashnikov slung across his shoulder.

'We'll make a detour. This way,' she continued guiding me across the street. 'Don't want to lead our friend to a den of iniquity.'

We had walked the length of the compound before making a loop and finally were following a sandy passage leading to the back entrance of John's house. Inside the place was buzzing with voices and the entire dimly lit lounge area bathed in a haze of smoke. Small groups were gathered round a makeshift bar while to one side the darts enthusiasts were in full swing. Knowing my intention was not to play darts Paula steered me towards the bar where a lanky British male was leaning on the counter and cradling a tankard of beer in his huge hand.

He turned to greet us with a lop-sided smile. He had a rather crumpled appearance giving the impression that he'd just stepped out of a tumble drier but his manner was friendly and easy. A glass of homemade sparkling white wine in my hand I learned that he had already visited some Roman sites including Sabratha and was eager to explore the desert. Just minutes later, after exchanging stories, Simon announced that he had a contact who could get return air tickets to the ancient desert city of Ghadames – an oasis settlement some 640 km southwest of Tripoli.

As I assured Simon that I was prepared to risk the well-publicised dangers of flying to get to the sand-mud desert city, I could feel a bulb of excitement growing inside. He was offering to organise the air tickets and promised to get in touch with me as soon as he had secured them.

****

A weekend in the desert was on the horizon. I tempered my excitement by reminding myself that this was Libya and nothing was certain. Getting hold of air tickets was one problem – the safety of flying in Libya was another. For a start there were no international flights and the remaining aircraft, used for internal flights, were suffering from lack of maintenance and parts. Prior to the renewed sanctions, which took effect from the first of December, French airline staff had serviced Libyan aircraft. The difficulty of getting replacement parts since the first sanctions were imposed in 1991, added to the dangers of flying.

In fact, stories about the problems of flying were rife. In December 1992 one of Libya's eight remaining Boeings crashed. All the passengers and crew were lost although the pilot and co-pilot had miraculously survived. Since the sanctions, French service engineers had been withdrawn and the dangers of flying in Libya had increased to such an extent that some oil companies had undertaken great road-building projects across the desert and now used road transport only into the desert sites. At that time, six of the original eight Boeings were in use. Rumour has it that number seven was being used for spare parts. Most individuals weren't prepared to risk flying. If I want to do something badly enough I ignore danger. Simon, I was to learn, behaved as if danger didn't exist.

Simon paid his contact for tickets and we waited for two weeks. Then the day before we expected to leave our money was returned. No tickets and no reasons. Simon believed that we would be able to purchase them ourselves at an airline office on our way to the airport. Nobody else did. In fact, long-term expatriate residents, including members of the Darts' Club were full of gloom and doom warnings and ultimatums. We remained steadfast.

There had been storms for several days and the morning we were due to leave I woke to no electricity and no running water though a deluge was falling outside. My head was alive with warnings: Simon's impracticability, the dangers of flying, the weather, reports of recent murders of tourists near the Algerian border – Ghadames is within sight of the border; the problems of getting hold of tickets had exacerbated as a result of restrictions imposed on expatriates since the sanctions. Finally, there was my CIA status. Although by now I was convinced that we wouldn't get away, I decided to leave it to fate. If we got the tickets and the flight, we'd go. In preparation I'd locked away my forbidden possessions: laptop, printer, disks, some American dollars. One thing was certain, Simon would be waiting for me. I got up by candlelight, packed my bag and set off into the gloom of a dark February morning.

The arrangement was that Simon's driver would to take us to an airline office to purchase our tickets and then drop us at the airport. The odds were against us: the weather was not on our side, phones weren't working and the driver was forty minutes late. By the time we set off we should have been checking in at the airport. I had convinced myself that it wasn't going to happen. Simon was unnervingly silent. It was still raining heavily. The streets were flooded. Swirling fetid water was filling the clogged drains with even more litter and sand. Then, in the way that life has of suddenly changing direction, we found ourselves at the airline office with tickets in our hands. Moments later, whooping with joy and congratulating ourselves we were heading for the airport.

Halfway there and still jubilant we faced a *volte-face*. The driver decided he didn't want to take us – the ten-kilometre journey was too far. His long unshaven face, dissatisfied expression and unkempt appearance did not inspire confidence. I could feel bottled up frustration and mild hysteria rising, and started remonstrating and pleading:

'We'll miss the flight – you can't dump us here in the rain!'

Simon remained stolidly calm. 'Heading in the right direction,' he muttered.

Then on a major roundabout on the outskirts of Tripoli the driver slowed down and kept his hand on the horn to get the attention of a taxi-driver about to overtake us. Amidst screeching brakes both vehicles pulled over to the side of the road. Simon leapt out. Ankle deep in flood water he was bargaining with the taxi driver. Water dripping from his nose and chin he signalled to me to get out. We transferred our baggage through the downpour and skidding traffic into the taxi.

Half an hour later we were at the wrong (international) airport. Fifteen minutes later we were at the right (domestic) airport. Fortunately, flight times are not take-off times in Libya but subject to the will of Allah and today Allah was on our side. With mixed feelings of elation and trepidation, I once again abandoned myself to fate, trailed Simon through the grey space serving as a departure lounge and joined the body of Libyan males surging towards the waiting aircraft.

The plane was not one of the remaining and dreaded 727 Boeings but, according to Simon, one of the less can go wrong variety – a twin engine Fokker – F27. It sounded like a tractor and taxied along and round overgrown airstrips for so long I thought that the entire journey was to be overland. Then with a sudden surge of speed, an increase in noise and the sight of the huge wheels lifting and folding like the legs of an enormous grasshopper I was convinced. We were airborne.

There were no safety instructions or seat belts never mind such luxuries as lifejackets and oxygen masks. Neither were there any restrictions on smoking. As soon as we took off the body of Libyan passengers lit up filling the cabin with a whirling noxious haze. Services on the one and a half hour flight included a boiled sweet at take off and a few minutes later, a drink. The air steward carried a tray of plastic cups half-filled with tepid water, tea-bags and a bowl of sugar. The alternative refreshment was coke. I passed on the refreshments and turned my attention to the view.

The cushion of heavy cloud that had obscured the fertile coastal plain gradually dispersed and I was looking down on the vertical edge of a vast red plateau – the frayed edges looked as if they had been nibbled by a huge monster. As we moved further south the red wasteland was traced by dried-up water courses lined by trees: tiny black blobs like the markings on an exquisitely drawn map. Simon's long legs stretched towards the aisle. His eyes were closed and his face wore the expression of a contented cat. Laughter lines radiated from his eyes and the corners of his lips tip-tilted in the expression of an eternal optimist. Over six feet tall with a moth-eaten haircut he was as easily distinguishable in a crowd as a tourist or a spy as I was with my blonde hair.

Minutes later, a young fresh-faced Libyan dressed in a spotlessly clean white *jalabiya* (loose, full length garment) and with a brown woollen cape casually draped about his shoulders came forward to take the spare seat next to us. Simon opened his eyes, withdrew and folded his legs into the space in front of him.

Introducing himself as Abu Bakr, the Libyan then informed us that he had been born and grew up in Ghadames and now ran the tourist office. He offered his services as a guide. Our exchanged glances indicated that we both knew that security was on our trail. We had been warned. Like expatriates, tour guides in Libya have a dual role. While we double up as tourists – they double up as security agents. As soon as he retreated we exchanged *sotto-voce* comments.

'What do you think?' Simon asked.

'We've been earmarked.'

'Travelling with a CIA agent is a risky business.'

'But interesting?'

'Certainly not dull.'

'At least we have a guide.'

'Native of Ghadames.'

'Sounds okay to me.'

'Sounds good.'

'At least we know where we are if you see what I mean?'

'I agree.' Simon concluded. 'Let's make the most of it.'

An hour later, under a pale sun looking as fragile as a glass globe, we landed on a desert airstrip surrounded by mile upon mile of red sand capped by endless blue sky. Two elongated, flat-topped hills, standing above the arid plain were the only focus on which the eyes could rest. The airport, a square featureless concrete building, consisted of one main room with a counter, a weighing machine and a row of orange plastic chairs. Baggage was delivered outside from the back of a vehicle, rather like a cement mixer disgorging its contents. Abu Bakr was waiting and had organised a lift for the ten kilometre drive to the only hotel in Ghadames. Simon gave a discreet thumbs-up sign. The smile on his lips said it all.

An Arab legend would have us believe that in the seventh century AD when the Arab conqueror, Okba Ibn Nafa, arrived at Ghadames exhausted from the heat, his mare pawed the earth with her hoof – a spring gushed from that very spot. Spring of the Mare: Ain Al Faras. This was the name given to the hotel.

Wheels crunching over the forecourt we drew up to a row of dusty palms standing guard against terracotta walls. Built by the Italians, over half a century ago, the hotel boasted traditional features of Saharan architecture including sand-based brickwork with a pattern of open triangles along the top of the walls and traditional pointed, raised stones at the corners of the buildings. During the Italian era Sophia Loren is reputed to have stayed at the hotel and more recently, Mark Thatcher, while taking part in the Paris-Dakar Car Rally in the days before Libya was boycotted. More importantly, the hotel was literally on the very doorstep of the ancient city.

Inside the building was dark, shabby and cold. An even darker lounge attached to the reception area was crowded with sagging velour armchairs all peopled by Libyan males wearing drab robes and long lengths of material bandaged about their heads. Rapid eye movement from and back to a mammoth television mounted on a table in one corner – the only indication of interest in our presence – made it difficult to tell if the reaction was one of indifference or antagonism. The room stank of full ashtrays and was dominated by strident tones issuing from the black and white speckled screen.

MEALS FOR REQUEST, printed in large letters on a placard, drew our attention to an otherwise empty reception counter. Eventually, one of the slouched figures rose from his armchair, stubbed out a half-smoked cigarette and made his way unceremoniously towards us. We swapped employment cards for keys and waited while our details were painstakingly jotted into a book.

The hotel formed a quadrangle round a courtyard as shabby and neglected as the building. Withered vines hung from a broken trellis; a dry fountain was spewing litter. A hibiscus with crumpled red blooms was the only near-living thing in the flowerbeds. Even the hardy date palms looked bedraggled. On either side of a central pathway fallen plastic tables and chairs were carelessly strewn over a lawn of sandy hillocks. I followed a track leading behind the trellis to number thirty-nine, wracking my brains for some explanation of the significance of the number. All I could come up with was John Buchan's thriller: *The Thirty-nine Steps*, and our lives as shades of the adventures of a man on the run. We weren't exactly on the run I consoled myself though the sense of being pursued was never far away. Simon was heading to the opposite side. A rather extreme form of gender separation, I presumed.

Cold inhabited the room – penetrating and tactile. There were three narrow beds. Each had a hard foam pillow, a thin sheet over the mattress and one folded blanket. An ancient air-conditioner boxed in a rusty cage; electric points rudely inserted in walls yellow with age while a switch hanging from a hole in the wall, operated an ugly strip-light straddling the ceiling.

I crossed the stone floor, tracing a sour smell to the adjoining bathroom and tested the plumbing: tepid water spluttered then trickled from taps but failed to operate in the bidet or toilet. A plastic bucket standing on the floor was on offer for do-it-yourself flushing. There were no plugs in the basin or bath. Sophia Loren here! It was impossible to imagine. Although winter and near freezing it was warmer outside in the last light of the pale swollen sun. I picked up my camera. Evening light was a good time to get some shots.

Pausing in the courtyard to lean against a pillar in slanting sunlight, I saw Simon striding towards me.

'Not exactly the Ritz,' I greeted him.

'Not exactly.'

'Verging on squalid, I'd say.'

'At least cold kills germs.'

'At least we're here.'

'Feels great.'

'Feels like adventure.'

'Worth the risk.'

'Worth ignoring born again pessimists.'

'Let's go then. This way!' Simon directed gesturing grandly to the start of a track just a few metres from the hotel.

I followed in his wake eventually arriving at an open space which looked down on the oasis – the starting point for the settlement at Ghadames – a city so ancient that historians believe it was inhabited 4,000 years ago. Natural springs are found in oases throughout the desert regions of Libya. Settlements like Ghadames have grown up around them and caravan routes have used them as stopping points since pre-Roman times. The Greek philosopher Strabo likened North Africa to a leopard's skin, its habitable areas being scattered like spots over a background of waterless desert.

The fifth century Greek historian Herotodus frequently draws attention to the diurnal and seasonal changes in water temperature, so characteristic of desert springs, as well as to their whereabouts for without their sweet water life and travel could not exist. Ghadames existed because of the availability of underground water. Walled in and with no visible surface water, walls of sand sloped to a circle of palms, grasses and shrubs hinting at its underground presence. The outer sections of the city fanned out between a series of passages running between high sand-mud walls from which, I estimated, it would have been possible to see over from the back of a camel. A distinctive feature of the architecture was the rows of bricks, in the shape of fat tiles, placed side by side along the tops of walls like books on a shelf. They ran across open land, divided by a network of low walls into overgrown enclosures that once held crops and animals.

Just past the oasis we came to an open area circled by tiers of seats or steps – the market and meeting place and a starting point for travellers and merchants, their camels packed with ivory, gold, ostrich feathers, slaves and wild animals before the last stage of the long journey north to the Mediterranean. I followed Simon climbing the steps to a central point from where we looked down on the square. In the absolute silence it was not difficult to imagine the tinkle of caravan bells as the long procession of camels arriving from Niger or Chad shuffled to a standstill. Above this the excitement of traders' greetings and bargaining overriding the stench of fear of shackled slaves and caged animals destined for the arenas of Libya's Roman cities as well as for the magnificent city of Rome itself.

Now, in the deserted quiet, disturbed only by our own footsteps, we rejoined the pathway passing a fort with high walls punctuated by randomly placed tiny square holes serving as windows. The traditional raised cornerstones, believed by local people to keep ghosts away, marked the top corners of the highest buildings and turrets. Ahead of us the outline of a tower and the small dome of a mosque glared white against cerulean sky; sunlight painted one side of the buildings gold and cast long shadows on the other. A dove was cooing. Cameras clicked and whirred.

A sandy passage lead through an archway and into an open courtyard – a daytime suntrap with a series of arched niches cut into the walls providing comfortable windproof seating. On one side was the entrance to the mosque and on the other the entrance to the men's living quarters. An arcaded portico led into a maze of tunnels that connect and interconnect the ground floor rooms of the entire city: the male preserve as dark and intricate as a network of rabbits' burrows.

We felt our way through the thick darkness of a tunnel coming across sudden gaps in the wall where more passages fed off to right and left. Ahead, a shaft of light guided us to the next courtyard. By the time we emerged from the underworld, as mysterious as any one of Italo Calvino's *Invisible Cities,* the sun had slipped out of sight. Brilliant stars were sprayed across the sky. The air tingled with the frost of a desert night.

As soon as we reached the hotel we made for the bar. There was a choice of stewed, sweet tea or coffee thick enough to keep a spoon upright. I settled for syrupy tea. The morgue-cold dining room, adjoining the bar, was furnished with a stained floral carpet and small tables covered with plastic cloths. Too late we discovered the importance of the 'Meals For Request' notice at reception. We hadn't requested meals therefore, no food was available. There was no standing on ceremony here. At that moment, our security agent-cum-guide, now in the guise of a guardian angel, glided up and offered to take us to a local Tuareg cafe in the village. Simon winked. We were realising the benefits of our self-appointed escort.

The café was rustic, filled with small wooden tables and crowded with men all wearing the distinctive swathed headgear of the legendary nomadic Berber warriors of the Sahara: the Tuareg. Outstanding for their long robes, embroidered sheaths for their weapons and swift Mehari camels, the Tuareg are especially recognisable by the *tagulmust* – the long strip of cotton cloth which they wrap round their heads, necks, chest, chin, and face up to the eyes to protect them from sand-laden desert winds.

The Tuareg reputation of being the fierce guardians of the Sahara has been substantiated by the accounts of a number of early explorers. The nineteenth century traveller and scholar Heinrich Barth on his travels from northern Cameroon to Mali was not alone in so fearing them that he:

... felt obliged to adopt the character of a Mohammedan, in order to traverse with some degree of safety the country of the Tawarek (Tuareg), and to enter the town of Timbuktu...[3]

More recently the Tuareg in Libya gave the colonial French in Algerià a hard time by conducting countless raids over the border. In spite of their fearsome reputation the atmosphere in the café was informal and friendly. Although no attempts were made to communicate verbally eye contact, smiles and body language were warm and we both felt unexpectedly at ease – something we had not experienced in the environs of Tripoli or indeed in the hotel. Dressed in their traditional long robes topped by windcheaters and with the casually wrapped and knotted *tagulmust* on their heads, they appeared both charming and rakish. We joined them in a palatable meal of couscous served with chicken legs and Arabic bread.

At nine o'clock the next morning the sun was shining, the air tinged with frost and the hotel dead. I was standing in the reception area dreaming of an enormous pot of tea when the manager appeared. I reminded him that we had ordered breakfast.

---

[3] Heinrich Barth, *Travels & Discoveries in North and Central Africa*

'Ramadan,' was his brusque explanation. Then, in response to my stunned silence, 'Arabs don't eat.'

His dead pan expression confirmed my fear and answered my silent reply: We're not Arabs. There were indeed no concessions for tourists. Dismayed, I realised that the first sliver of the new moon heralding the start of the month of fasting, must have been sighted last night. The remains of snacks I'd packed for the journey would have to suffice until sundown this evening. This, in turn jolted my memory and the 'Meals For Request' notice. We'd have to order now for the evening meal. With this in mind I set off to find Simon.

At ten o'clock precisely, as he had promised, Abu Bakr arrived wearing the lugubrious expression adopted by Arab males when fasting. Nevertheless, he looked handsome in his long striped gown and woollen cape. After his customary greeting of 'Hallo how are you fine?' he led us along the track we'd taken last evening into the old city. As we walked he explained that his family had moved out in 1979 and that by 1984 every family from the old city had to evacuate – an estimated 8,000 people were re-housed in the new town.

It is rumoured that fearing that the old city was a place of intrigue and impossible to watch the 'Powers' authorised the building of a new and modern housing complex for the inhabitants and directed the complete evacuation of the old settlement. The reluctance of some families to move was still evident. As if the city were still alive we were passed by a constant stream of people: a boy carrying a goat; two elderly men, wrapped in cream *baracans* (cloaks) and out for a stroll in the sun; an elderly couple – the woman bent over by the weight of a bundle of dried grass tied across her back while her husband strolled unencumbered at her side. She was pulling at the end of her striped *farashiya* (long strip of material covering the head and shoulders) in an attempt to hide her entire face. An old man, carrying a walking stick, moved briskly along the passage as if he had business to attend to.

'Old men like come back,' Abu Bakr explained. 'Visit home. Pray at mosque.'

In an open courtyard near the entrance to the 'underground' houses two elderly men were sitting in the sun. One, wearing a large pair of modern spectacles looked especially vulnerable and caught between two worlds.

'*Bonjour,*' his companion called. '*Ca Va?*' adding yet another dimension to the mixture of time, place and cultures.

Abu Bakr's clean-shaven, oval face was as expressionless as the tone he adopted to describe the everyday customs and way of his former life. His one reference to the distant past:

'Before Arab four different tribe live in city' – was left tantalisingly in mid-air. Only when we pressed him did he satisfy our curiosity by explaining that two main tribes once lived in the city, the Bani Walid and his people, the Bani Wazid. While the Bani Walid lived in three separate but interconnecting sections of the city his tribe, he confided, occupied four. The main square was for all the people. The Tuareg, he explained, were new comers to Ghadames. It wasn't until recent years that some of them gave up their nomadic lifestyles and set up homes in new quarters to the east of the city.

With its natural supplies of spring water and growing opportunities as a trading centre, Ghadames would have been a convenient place for Berber tribal groups to gravitate to and set up permanent homes. Strategically located at the northernmost point of the Tuareg domain, Ghadames became a vital last stop of the trans-Saharan caravans en route to the Mediterranean; it was here that the highest prices for slaves were paid in the local market. Then in the eighteenth and nineteenth centuries when the trade in slaves was in decline the Tuareg changed course from slave traders to slave owners. They enslaved black Africans as their servants to tend their livestock and gardens and to perform domestic duties in their homes.

It is said that to this day, home to the majority of the Tuareg remains within the limitless reaches of the Sahara. Fiercely independent, they describe themselves as 'noble and free'; they recognize no boundaries, obey no laws. Political tensions of the mid-1990s, that ended when cease fires were signed with Niger and Mali, have reignited. The Tuareg took up arms when an increase in cattle tax was imposed. The invisible boundaries of their territories, where the Sahel meets the green fields and villages of settled agriculturalist Bantu people, are where age-old hostilities continue to take place. At times of severe drought the Tuareg gravitate towards the Niger to water and feed their herds and to find food for themselves. This is when the hatred between the Tuareg and the sedentary people flares; denied freedom of access to fertile watered lands north of the river, the Tuareg not only burn villages and steal livestock but enslave the people.

On his travels through Mali the Polish writer and foreign correspondent, Ryskard Kapuscinski, asked a man from Mopti where he could meet the Tuareg. The guy looked at him with pity and disbelief. Kapuscinski was taken to see the remains of a Mali fishing village recently destroyed by the Tuareg. Local people, he was told, regard the Tuareg as the terrorists of the Sahara.

In spite of the 1971 law abolishing slavery in Mali members of the Bella tribe remain as slaves to the Tuareg in all but name. When asked why, the Bella's response is the response of a number of African tribes when questioned about why they continue with sometimes brutal customs: 'It is tradition. It is our culture or it has always been this way.' On her visit to Timbuktu, in 2001, the indomitable solo traveller, Kira Salak, paid a Tuareg master for the freedom of two of his female slaves.

We followed Abu Bakr into one of the tunnels into the city. As our eyes grew accustomed to the thick darkness he stopped to point to one of the heavy palm wood doors where a row of small pieces of leather had been nailed to the surface.

'Each time man travel he nail leather to door.' Abu Bakr explained. 'This tell friend and neighbour he go away.'

That the pieces of tell-tale leather remained in place gave a sense of immediacy to the recent past as well as a sense of loss. Built long before designs were committed to paper each door differed in some way from its neighbour – the very asymmetry of the designs remains part of the attraction. From time to time we emerged from the interconnecting tunnels into the bright sunlight of a courtyard – one was once the market place another led to an Islamic school. This, Abu Bakr believed, was the first school in Ghadames.

It is possible that at one time a Christian school may have existed in the city. Among their converts to Catholicism the Byzantines included people of *Cydamae* (Ghadames). In fact, it is said that between the fourth and fifth centuries Ghadames, an episcopate under the Byzantine Empire, was served by four bishops. Columns, capitals and pieces of masonry used in the mosque have been identified as the remains taken from the former Christian basilica.

Though nominally Muslim, the Tuareg retain a number of pre-Islamic rights and customs including that of insisting that the men wear veils while the women remain unveiled. Claims of their former Christian beliefs have been supported by the importance of the symbol of the cross in their culture: notably in the jewellery, the Agadez Cross on their swords and shields and in the unique design of the saddle: a circular seat which rests on a V-shaped frame. While the back end of the frame is marked by a finger-like point, the upward front curve is fashioned into the shape of a cross. We had the good fortune to see one close up, propped on a wall with the distinct form of a cross silhouetted like a crucifix against the sky. The question remains: was the conversion of the Tuareg to Islam the result of 'Kissing the Hand'[4] to avoid death or slavery at the hands of proselytising, sword wielding Arabs?

A fascinating pen and ink drawing shows the celebrated German traveller Heinrich Barth's Tuareg guide holding a crucifix in one hand while sitting aloft a camel draped with a cloth marked with a cross as distinctive as those worn by Crusaders. In fact, Barth thought the word Tuareg came from the Arabic: *tereju dinihum,* meaning 'they changed their religion'. All intriguing stuff. That change in religious belief went hand in hand with a fanatical intolerance towards 'unbelievers' is undisputed.

Catholic missionaries from the Society of White Fathers in Algeria – established in Tripoli and Ghadames from 1878-1881 – planned to set up further missions in West Africa, travelling via Ghat into Niger and the Sudan. The story told is that in December 1881 three White Fathers set off from Ghadames accompanied by five Tuareg guides. Before reaching Ghat they were assassinated by the Tuareg. They were not alone in receiving this fate at the hands of the Tuareg. The Scottish Explorer, Gordon Laing was just one of a number of European explorers to suffer a similar fate for refusing to renounce their Christian faith and convert to Islam. It was literally more than a traveller's life was worth to refuse their 'favours' as escorts through the desert. Barth was one of the few travellers who discovered that the Tuareg's religious fervour diminished when offered a substantial portion of his expedition goods.

Just minutes later, Abu Bakr was in conversation with a man who had been hiding in an empty room. Learning that he was Algerian and had no passport, he left him to his own devices. It was a jolt into the present and an uncomfortable reminder of the closeness of the

---

[4] Tuareg saying: 'Kiss the hand you cannot sever'.

border with the current spate of Islamic fundamental violence against foreigners.

We left the courtyard and joined a passageway where we heard, then saw a fast-running stream of water fed by a natural freshwater spring: the legendary 'Spring of the Mare'. Water from this spring, once used to irrigate the fields of the oasis and now channelled to the houses of the new town is said to be warm in winter and cold in summer. Abu Bakr invited me to test it. Hand-warm and perfectly clear it explained the one luxury available at the hotel – warm tap water.

Finally, we entered another tunnel. Stopping in front of a large palm wood door Abu Bakr handed Simon a metal key some six inches long. 'Place for woman. Man downstair. Woman upstair. Open door!' he instructed.

'Feels wrong,' Simon muttered, 'like breaking and entering into a nunnery.'

The key clunked in the lock, the door creaked as it opened onto a darkened stone stairway. Once Abu Bakr had locked us in we followed him up the steps emerging onto a middle floor used as the main living area. Although deliberately set up as a museum it was impressive. Red was the dominant colour – in the rugs and cushions covering the floors; lengths of material draped across walls and in the traditional three triangle designs painted on walls and over cupboards; two smaller doors opened onto recesses in the wall. Rows of small brass dishes and brass-framed mirrors decorated the walls. Light coming from the only window – an opening in the roof, reflected off the white walls and refracted from mirrors illuminating the room.

At one end, behind a curtain, was the marriage bed furnished with especially rich rugs and embroidered bolster covers while two more areas where the women and children slept were divided off by curtains.

'Boys,' Abu Bakr explained, 'live with woman until twelve or thirteen – after they live with father downstairs.'

A set of wooden steps led up to a small and austere room reserved for the grandfather. Apart from a bed, his only comfort was a large copy of the Quran lying open on a stand. Men, it seemed, spent their final days of their lives in the upper storeys, their needs attended to by the women.

A second flight of stairs led to rooms for storing food, washing and cooking. In the kitchen there were two deep, oval, stone hollows for kneading bread. Baking and cooking were done over fires made from the thick stems of palm fronds and laid in hollows between a row of small stone domes on which cooking utensils were balanced. Colourful food covers, like huge conical straw hats, adorned the walls. The largest specimen was placed over a huge couscous pot. Pointing to a sealed opening in the wall Abu Bakr explained that is was a place to store grain. Nearby, a second hole, which plummeted to ground level, was used as a chute for waste.

Finally, we were standing on the flat interconnecting roof-top of the city. Here, on the top levels of the building the women could meet and talk together. Just as the men's passages interconnected beneath so their rooftops provided them with access to all the upper roofs of the houses in the city. In his expressionless tone, Abu Bakr explained that women were allowed down to the lower level twice each day, morning and evening, when the men were at prayer in the mosque, to get water for washing and cooking.

'Before prayer finish they come back,' he added.

Simon and I exchanged glances. 'You mean,' queried Simon, 'except to get water the women were not allowed downstairs, not allowed to walk outside.'

'They have roof,' Abu Bakr persisted, then conceded, 'Sometime woman walk with husband.'

Silenced by his phlegmatic response we followed him down the stairs into the sunlight. The feeling of sand beneath my feet, sunlight streaming through passages leading to the oasis and the freedom to walk through them took on an entirely new perspective.

The use of courtyards, enabling each extended family group – male, female, young and old – to have its own safe meeting places for recreation and relaxation, was a long established Eastern tradition. This morning it had been made clear that the arrival of Islam and its insistence on gender separation, taken to an extreme in Ghadames, had irrevocably changed the nature of family and social life for the women of this ancient desert city. The origins and reasons remained unclear. Had the arrival of Islam and its insistence of gender separation practised in Ghadames been taken to an extreme? Or were the women of this labyrinthine city being protected from slave traders and invading foreign armies? Whatever the origin that the practice continued over the centuries to end less than ten years ago, when the old city was evacuated, was difficult to come to terms with.

I was still contemplating the plight of the women when on our way back to the hotel we passed two local females. Completely wrapped in striped cotton *farashiyas* they held the ends across their faces, revealing one eye in a neat triangular gap. It was difficult not to apply western judgements and feel terrible compassion for these women who, released from a life-time of restriction to the rooftops of the city less than ten years ago, were now restricted to viewing the outside world with one eye. It was also a sobering reminder that centuries of oppression take more than a handful of decades to overcome.

Sandra and Eric, two Swiss adventurers staying with embassy friends in Tripoli, joined us in the afternoon. The freedom to invite friends and family to visit them in Libya was just one of a number of advantages enjoyed by embassy staff.

'Sounds like pure punishment.' was Simon's response when he learnt the couple had travelled 640 kilometres along a desert track by bus to reach Ghadames.'

'We were told that to fly would be tantamount to a death-wish.'

'I've heard the buses aren't much safer.'

'A nightmare night-ride,' Sandra confirmed. 'Long, rough and smoke-filled. I daren't think about the return.'

'I don't want to add to your misery but there's no food till sundown. Ramadan is upon us. No concessions for tourists.'

'Now, we can help on that one. Our friends in Tripoli were prepared and have set us up with a picnic. We'll be happy to share.'

While we helped demolish supplies of Arabic bread, *homous*, chicken legs and salad we discovered the plans for the afternoon's run to a desert lake and a Roman fort. First stop was Lake Tumin – a salt lake in the desert once important for the supply of rushes used for the walls and roofs of desert homes.

With Abu Bakr as our guide and a Tuareg driver, swathed in a romantic tagulmust – looking as at home behind the wheel of the ancient Land Cruiser as he would have done on a camel – we set off into the desert. There was an air of elation and expectation as we headed for the red, rocky desert of *Hammadah al Hamra* – known and feared as an area of impenetrable desolation, it was a region crossed by the Roman armies in expeditions against the warring Garamantes tribe. All too soon the tarmac road we'd been following disappeared beneath drifting sand and a line of miniature rippled dunes and we were heading across a featureless gravel plain.

Following ruts, rather like those left by tractors across previously sodden but now baked fields, our route was taking us on a course running parallel to the foot of a low-lying escarpment some fifty metres on our left. The surface of the great plain, dotted with boulders, was becoming increasingly white with crusted salt – as if there had been a light fall of snow or a hoar frost. Finally, a line of shrubs marked an underground watercourse, then a flash of blue.

'Did you see that?' Sarah called hopefully. 'Looked like water.'

In the distance I too caught a glimpse of what could have been a mirrored patch of sky reflected in the waters of a lake. Held between a break in a ring of trees it appeared to be cradled in the centre of a small hill straight ahead of us. However, distances are as deceptive in the desert as at sea and the seemingly endless jarring and trundling over stony desert to reach our goal took so long that I feared what we had seen was no more than a mirage or wishful thinking. Finally, the vehicle did slow and we drew to a standstill at the foot of the hill.

Out of the vehicle we had our first experience of trudging through deep soft sand to reach the top of the ridge circling the lakes. The effort of the sinking and lifting of feet reminded me of trudging through snow with similar feelings of anticipation. Finally, we were standing on the crest overlooking three interconnecting lakes cupped in a hollow. Some 100 metres wide the lakes were protected by a ring of shrubs, trees and rushes that grew from the soft hills of sand surrounding it. The main, central lake said to reach to a depth of thirty-five metres, reflected the blue of the sky and fed two shallow interconnecting pools on either side from overflow channels. Crouching on the shoreline I gazed through crystal clear water. I could see quite clearly plants with waving fronds growing two to three metres down the vertical sides while the centre was a deep impenetrable green.

'People use rush for house, mat, basket, shoe – many thing. After dark they afraid,' Abu Bakr explained. 'Believe strange creature live in water. People not come after dark.'

A small Roman castle was next on our itinerary. Along with several larger forts, established in the second century, its purpose was to help deal with attacks from desert tribes in an attempt to bring the pre-desert firmly within the Empire. We were trundling west across the same red featureless desert with occasional patches of scrub and salt marking the remains of a dry water course and straight into the eye of the fast descending sun. Low winter sunlight dazzled and burned through the windows hinting at its full summer power when temperatures reached well over fifty degrees in the shade. Suddenly, the desert-red, camouflaged castle capping a small hill rose before us like a sleepy dinosaur.

As soon as we were at a standstill Abu Bakr was out of the vehicle, striding towards a well at the foot of the hill and pointing to the entrance to a tunnel alongside it. 'Secret way to castle,' was his explanation.

On his hands and knees Simon was peering into the semi-collapsed opening, not unlike an entrance to a fox's lair. His head and shoulders disappeared briefly before he reluctantly backed out, rubbing sand from his hair and giving up on an impulse to reach the castle through the tunnel. From where we were standing at the foot of the hill, the perfectly camouflaged sand-coloured stones of the castle walls appeared to grow out of and be part of the mound it capped.

Buffeted by strong winds we scrambled up and involuntarily slithered down a steep winding path, slippery with lose sand and stones until breathless and eager we were hauling each other up the stone ramparts of the remaining curtain wall which once circled the castle.

Positioning ourselves along the western ramparts, we enjoyed panoramic views to a row of magnificent dunes. From this vantage point the strategic importance of the Ghadames became clear. Poised like eagles in the safety of their eyrie, the Romans had clear views across uninterrupted miles of stony desert plains. The approach of caravans with their precious loads or invading tribes from any direction could be seen long before they arrived. Not only did the castle give the Romans an excellent vantage point for detecting any movement or approach from across the Algerian border – it also enabled them to impose taxes and control trade at this strategic position.

Haynes tells us that occasional coalitions of tribes fought against the Romans and that in AD 547 three great tribes, each ruled by kings: the Ifuraces, the Garamantes of the Fezzan and the Nasamones from Syrte, attacked the Tripolitanian coast before launching a surprise attack on the Byzantines, who had followed them into the desert, inflicting severe defeat on them.

The Romans weren't the only invaders to be resisted by indigenous people. Although contemporary Arab Libyans prefer to see their predecessors as fraternal settlers warmly welcomed by local people when they arrived in Libya the reality is very different. Haynes states that Arab invaders were strongly resisted by indigenous tribes:

... great Berber tribal groups of medieval Tripolitania emerge. In particular, the Nefusa and Huoara were later to contend bitterly with the Arabs for possession of their country...[5]

---

[5] D. E. L. Haynes, *The Antiquities of Tripolitania*

Driven into the Jabal by invading Arabs, the Berber people developed troglodyte dwellings into defensive citadels. Although, eventually abandoned, some not until the 1970s when families continued to return to escape the extreme heat of summer – the recognizable ruins of these Berber strongholds stand on peaks of the Jabal to this day. As late as 1911, when the Italians arrived in Libya, tribal resistance to invaders was such that it took the Italians three years to gain a foothold in Ghadames. When they finally arrived, such was their love of the ancient city that they treated the Ghadamsia with great sympathy and built the hotel, Ain al Faras, on its very doorstep. Today, the surrounding desert is an empty wasteland. Pointing to a gap in a row of trees, growing before a distant line of dunes and using his hand as a marker, Abu Bakr indicated: 'Algeria left: Tunisia right.'

Leaving the castle we headed south across the plain, the sun now drilling a hole through my window. There were an increasing number of shrubs and the occasional oasis, marked by a clump of palms, like islands in the ocean. Ahead of us stretched the meandering alluvial plain of a former river, wide enough to have been a great delta or a vast lake. Occasional sheets of white flashed like tin foil. It seemed as if with just a slight rise in the water table great stretches of the desert could turn into an inland sea or vast lake. One minute we were crossing flat ground and the next we were climbing a hillock of compact sand to find ourselves at the foothills of a line of awe-inspiring dunes. The low sun cast deep shadows emphasising the beauty and perfect symmetry of the huge crescent curves.

We soon discovered that there's nothing like dune climbing to take your breath away. Feet and legs disappearing under us as soft sand gave and rolled away we trudged breathless but joyful to a perfect knife-edge. The line defining the crest separated the two sides of the dune – one as smooth as milk – the other rippled like the held surface of a wind-blown lake. It was the absolute silence and sense of eternity that held us motionless. Lifted by a breeze, a veil of powdered sand, drifted, rested and took off again.

Libya 2014

Tragically, political turmoil in Libya continues to this day. The hope of peace in 2006, following Gaddafi's agreement to hand over the Lockerbie suspects and to eliminate his country's weapons of mass destruction programme, was short lived. Then, since the murder of Gaddafi in 2011 interim governments have faced multiple challenges and failed to control deteriorating security in the capital and other major cities. Libya is a land of regional, tribal, ethnic warlords who, all too often, are well-armed racketeers exploiting their power and the absence of an adequate police force. Reports continue of armed groups controlling security in many parts of the country, while thousands of detainees remain in government and militia controlled facilities without access to justice. Today, nobody is safe.

Sky High in the Emirates

My final overseas posting, in the United Arab Emirates, had many advantages. In fact, compared to the nightmare of Libya under sanctions, it was a gift. The speedy development of sky reaching tower blocks was a stark contrast to both the jungle surrounds of Brunei and Libya's desert plains. On a practical level – providing the 'rules' were obeyed – it was a safe, tax-free haven for work and leisure, plus a welcome relief to be released from the long soul and body-wearying flights, followed by jet lag, to and from Singapore and then beyond to Brunei. Less than eight hours away, as the swallow flies from home, the Emirates had the additional advantage of being closer to family and friends.

Once again I took every opportunity to escape the heat by sailing 470s at Abu Dhabi Sailing Club and as crew on various yachts at DOSC – Dubai Offshore Sailing Club. Membership of the local Natural History Group provided opportunities to take part in a number of expeditions into the then unspoilt surrounding desert, mountains and coastal regions. It was through these activities I met Richard (Chapman) – the owner of *Sunset Song*: a 35 foot sailing yacht and a remarkable and reliable Ssang-Yong Musso (4x4). From the start we were soul mates. I had a like-minded travel companion – one, I was soon to discover who, born and growing up in Rhodesia, was even more at home in the wilderness than I was.

A further advantage of the Emirates was the convenience of its position for further travels both into Asia as well as those throughout neighbouring Oman and into Central Africa – recorded in *Way South of Wahiba Sands*[6]. The poem *Khor Fakkan*, gives a sense of the unchanged world of the eastern Emirate of Fujairah at the turn of the century, where the BSAC Diving Group had the use of a villa for weekend dives: this also acts as a prelude to a visit to Nepal with Karen, expatriate colleague and friend, who invited me to join her trekking in the foothills of the Annapurna Mountains.

---

[6] *Way South of Wahiba Sands* (Austin Macauley, 2013)

Khor Fakkan

He left for Kathmandu, leaving her
a box of Cribari Burgundy, his mattress
and bedroll for comfort and protection from rats
in the villa at Khor Fakkan. She wondered
if diving in the Indian Ocean was worth the risk
of Leptospirosis? Just thinking about the list
of symptoms made her feverish.

More like a cowshed than a villa
she thought as she swept straw and rat-droppings
into the garden: a wilderness of saw-tooth palms
and banana plantains inhabited by chickens and goats.
She watched a rat test its footing on a rope,
skitter towards a dark hole.

A moonlight dive – mesmerised
by psychedelic ripples – streams of liquid silver
slipping across the ocean floor. Looking up
she watched her breath: a cascade of silver-coated
expanding bubbles rushing towards the moon.

That night she pulled the bedroll tight

about her, dreamed of rats with purple teeth.

Row upon row of purple mountains rise

from the desert floor: jagged rock pinnacles,

bare as bone picked clean – an impenetrable gleaming fortress.

At Dibba, fishermen place baby sharks

in rows upon the quay – sad mouths uppermost.

A heap of parrot-fish: glazed eyes in a sheen of blue,

lips parted over tightly closed beaks.

Martini Rocks: an underwater cathedral

of pinnacles and spires decked out in soft corals

of purple and lime-green.

Like a manic preacher a moray eel opens

and closes its jaws in silent admonition –

with a flourish unfolds like a silken ribbon.

A dithering pipe-fish hesitates between

congregating shoals and a procession of banner fish.

A nonchalant turtle passes.

Along the road

the miniature mosque's white turrets -

like tufts of whipped cream – a spider-web window

in each wall. Honey-coloured sun;

through a screen of trees, an ancient fort.[7]

---

[7] Al Bidyah Mosque: estimated to have been built in 1446, along with two nearby watch towers.

As she leaves the chain of polished mountains
the bald sun hanging in its scrubbed blue dome
she thinks of him in the verdant Himalayas
crowned with autumnal golds, snow-capped peaks
the sun erupting – red – from turbulent cloud,
crisp leaves falling – returns to the black tarmac road
snaking between naked dunes:
the aching emptiness of absence.

Staircase to Heaven

The bronze and green terraced slopes of the Kathmandu Valley rose to meet the aircraft as it lost height. Within minutes we were bouncing and rumbling over the airport's tarmac runway, struggling through controls and the minutiae of bureaucracy into an onslaught of locals armed with coloured brochures and vying with each other for the custom of the scattering of arrivals. They had no qualms about denouncing each other and were united and steadfast in their insistence that the Kathmandu Guesthouse was full. Karen and I had made reservations some weeks ago from our base in Abu Dhabi and were equally insistent in our determination to stay at the guesthouse. After extricating ourselves from our pursuers we made for the nearest clapped out vehicle, serving as a taxi, and were soon speeding towards the outskirts of Kathmandu.

The touts had not been far from the truth for the guesthouse was oversubscribed: cancelled flights for those expecting to leave meant that we had been downgraded to more modest accommodation than we had anticipated. However, we had a room, beds with clean sheets, the use of a shared loo and shower and the advantage of being conveniently situated to satisfy our plans: a visit to Chitwan National Park and a three-day trek through part of the Annapurna Range. Built round a central square where meals are served in the open, the guest house exuded an air of monastic simplicity and calm; it was a perfect retreat from the noise, colour and bustle of street vendors, tuk-tuks and thronging crowds – the essential life-force of Kathmandu.

First light saw us boarding a bus for the initial stage of our journey to the jungle island resort of Bandarjhola – an island nature reserve adjoining Chitwan National Park; some 90 km west of Kathmandu, the resort is the prime habitat of the Royal Bengal Tiger and a wide variety of big game including rhinos and elephants. However, there is nothing like a journey on local public transport to bring one down to earth: an overflow of passengers plus an overflow of luggage left the engine of the bus struggling; each time we hit a pot-hole a grinding noise was followed by belching blue fumes. Then as the suburbs of Kathmandu diminished and we rumbled along a track between encroaching overgrown verges the ride became more like a family outing than public transport. The driver chatted and joked with passengers, stopping at increasingly frequent intervals to let people on or off; to drop off or pick up packages or to chat with friends; on one occasion we all waited patiently while he disappeared into a thatched roadside house to enjoy a cup of tea.

Finally, we arrived at the pick-up point for a truck that was to take us through seven kilometres of riverine forest to Chitwan's Nature Reserve. As we neared the Narayani River, which splits and surrounds Bandarjhola Island, we passed through fields of rice and a village of bamboo thatched houses where families acknowledged our passing with friendly waves and smiles. At the river's edge a guide-cum-boatman was waiting in a rustic rowing boat to ferry us to the island; great trees crowded the waterside and lined a jungle pathway that took us to the resort. Following the guide, along a well-worn track beneath a canopy of moisture-dripping trees, I had an increasing sense of being in another time and another world. Then civilisation in the form of a huge open-sided, circular bamboo reception-cum-dining hall, set under an awning of trees with a ready prepared lunch of homemade bread and vegetable soup, welcomed us to this unique river island nature reserve.

Accommodation was in small thatched huts – the mud walls and ceilings lined with plaited bamboo or in tents under thatched awnings. In spite of the air of dampness, accentuated by moisture dripping from trees, we were both glad of the relative comfort of a thatched room. Kerosene lamps provided some lighting while power from a generator was used to light the dining hall.

The air of dampness that greeted our arrival was the start of an even damper afternoon. Loud and ominous cracks of thunder heralded our first activity – a tiger spotting elephant safari through jungle. Undeterred by impending rain we made our way to the specially erected mounting-stand and onto an ingenious contraption resembling an upturned wooden table tied to the elephant's back; this provided seating and support columns for four people. With mounts and passengers in position and handlers sitting astride the elephants' necks, legs and bare feet working non-stop directing and urging their charges forward, we set off into the gloom of the jungle.

Just minutes later, the first huge spots of rain were followed by a torrential downpour. As the forest became dark and unfriendly and expectations of sightings of tiger or rhino receded we were handed pink plastic sheets to hold over our heads. Huddled under my innovative umbrella, rivulets of water running down my neck and seeping through my clothes, I attempted to distract myself by watching the way the elephant splayed its toes before placing each foot on sodden ground and listening to the satisfying thud as its droppings landed. Speeded-up images of seeds taking root in steaming dung and growing into new forest trees filled my head.

*****

In the absolute silence of first light the river murmured beneath swathes of mist. Then it slowly lifted and above the ghostly shapes of trees the outline of the snow-capped peak of Mount Himalchuli – the second highest of three main peaks in the Nepalese Himalayas – was visible above cloud. Like an orchestra starting up, a frenzy of birdsong heralded sunrise reminding us that bird watching was on the agenda. Since neither of us was armed with binoculars – Karen chose to relax over a pot of coffee while I decided to tag along behind the bird-watchers on a jungle trail between huge buttress roots of towering trees.

I soon gave up looking for invisible birds and concentrated on shafts of sunlight filtering through leaves, catching the red glow of an occasional beetle through mounds of crystalline sand. I was mulling over the guide's instructions about what to do if one came face to face with a wild creature: rhino, he told us, run in a straight line so, to escape, we should run in a zigzag; on the other hand, one should stand perfectly still and look straight into the eyes of a tiger; however, when confronted by a bear, the best policy was to lie down and pretend to be dead. It was while I was contemplating the dubious outcome from any one of these responses that the guide suddenly stopped.

'Bird too high, too fast with no binocular,' he announced. 'We go to river.'

I followed in his footsteps stopping at the forest's edge to photograph distant snow-capped peaks when from across the water. 'Rhino!' a voice shouted. The cry was echoed by the guide who was already speeding towards the river. Given the right incentive my walking boots instantly transform into running shoes. I was sprinting after the guide along the riverbank, down to the water's stony edge. There, in the river, the head, twitching ears and back of a one-horned rhino were visible. Birds, perched on its shoulders, were nonchalantly pecking insects from its hide.

Meanwhile in an attempt to make the rhino emerge from the water the guide was experimenting with various encouraging calls and banging a pole against a dead tree. He assured me that in less than half an hour the rhino would come ashore to eat the long grass.

'Come,' he said. 'Follow me.'

Small, wiry and quick on his feet, he took off. I was back into sprinting mode, through trees and over roots, until we emerged at a spot on the river's bank. Opposite us on a small island was the rhino, as handsome as he was large. He took no notice of us. Keeping in mind the instructions to run a zigzag route if chased by a charging rhino, I took advantage of his apparent indifference by crossing the low water to the island, where he was feeding, to get some close-up shots.

Crocodiles were on the agenda for the afternoon. We followed a footpath through the forest to a clearing with a good view of a wide, shallow stretch of river. There, on the far side an adult crocodile was resting at the water's edge with a youngster lying alongside. The snout and eyes of another were just visible above the surface. 'Mugger,' the boatman enlightened us. As we got into the boat the muggers slid into the water. Further downstream baby crocodiles were snoozing on sandy islets. Overhead an eagle rested on lazy thermals. A chital deer was drinking at the water's edge. The plop of water from the boatman's lifted oars as he propelled us through the current was the only sound to break the silence.

Suddenly, we were startled by a tremendous high pitched squealing from the opposite bank. Then we saw a group of men wrestling with a pig. Minutes later a boat crossed our path with the inert body of the pig across its bows. There were no guesses about what was for supper that night. Back at the resort, with handlers riding Mowgli-style, elephants were crossing the river in time for the afternoon jungle safari – this time in sunlight.

Annapurna: Goddess of Harvests

Pokhara was the destination for the start of a three day trek in the foothills of the Annapurna Range. First we had to endure a six hour bus ride. There were no spare seats but everyone moved up and we managed to squeeze into the back row between a woman suckling her baby and a sleeping man. Heat, noise and congestion ruled. Through the window glimpses of a dramatic river gorge and snow-capped peaks reminded me of the wonders that lay ahead. We were booked into a guest house within easy walking distance of the beautiful Phew Lake; when we finally arrived we were delighted to find that it more than lived up to its reputation, with the added bonus that our room had views across the lake which acted as mirror to the mountains. Background music during the evening meal was the chanting of Buddhist monks – reminiscent of plainchant: a splendid setting to prepare us for the expedition.

Although I was excited at the opportunity of partaking in a mountain trek, as the moment for the start drew near I was beginning to suffer qualms. Rather like ski runs, treks are graded and the route from Phedi, through the foothills of the Annapurna Range, was supposed to be for beginners. However, after three hours of vertical rock climbing followed by a descent that punished the knees and tested the thighs, reality set in. Even with a porter carrying our backpacks the pattern of ascent and descent required total concentration on the next foothold and allowed no time for such luxuries as stopping to admire the view or to photograph a resting butterfly or even conversation. We passed through the villages of Dhampus then Pothana. I braced myself for one more steep descent then a final ascent to Tolka before we could collapse and rest for the night.

Breakfast on a terrace with splendid views of snow-capped peaks was the reward for yesterday's punishment but there was no time for lazing. By eight a.m. we were descending to Landruk and the Modi Khola River through a landscape of terraced hillsides and perilously perched farms to a tiny village school. Consisting of one room, with pillars of stone at each corner to support the wooden sides and roof, it too was suspended over the hillside. Inside it was furnished with three wooden benches on which were perched a dozen or so small wide-eyed children.

Back on the trail we were passed by a constant stream of local people: barefoot and carrying heavy loads they climbed or descended with enviable ease. I wobbled perilously across a swaying wooden slatted bridge over the river that marked the start of the ascent to Ghandruk. The final approach up a flight of stone steps, built into the mountain, was so high and so steep that the steps disappeared into blue sky making literal sense of a staircase to heaven. Taking a deep breath and determined to overcome thoughts of aching limbs by counting the steps, I began the three hour ascent. The reward: in evening light the stunning view of the fishtail peaks of Machhapuchhre were outlined by clear blue sky; beneath the mountains a brilliant bowl of white dropped behind terraced fields which glowed copper gold.

On a visit to Ghandruk's conservation centre we watched a video showing the draining of the Ganges Plain to create land for intensive rice farming and the way that this has impinged on wild life of the region. Problems arose because the rice fields encroach on the natural habitat of the one-horned rhino, the Bengal Tiger as well as

261

elephants. In turn, the protected wild animals destroy crops and prey on livestock. It has taken time but now the farmers and hill people are adapting to tourism and the need to preserve wild life and forests. Government funding helps them to convert barns for accommodation, provides solar panels for heating and taps for water, while electricity from generators helps to prevent the destruction of forests: positive actions to help the people and preserve wildlife habitats.

I was up at first light looking for the best viewing point from which to capture the stunning surroundings. Although it was almost November the gardens of the hotel were still awash with blossoms and flowers: the delicate pink of Japanese anemones, golden marigolds and orange, red and cerise blooms emerged from darkness. Terraced fields of rice and the farms of Ghandruk staggered up the hillside, beneath Machhapuchhre's luminescent peaks. As the sun appeared we enjoyed a breakfast of homemade muesli with hot milk, Tibetan bread and local honey and pots of milky tea in the hotel's garden.

It was on the descent to Birethanti we realised that the most scenically beautiful part of the entire trek was behind us. So much so that we spent a great deal of time stopping and turning round to absorb dramatic changes in scenery and absolutely breath-taking views of the snow-capped peaks of Annapurna. I resolved that should I return to Kathmandu I would trek in the opposite direction – from Birethanti towards Ghandruk and towards the mountains.

Now our downhill route took us towards the wide flood plain of the Modi Khola River; swathes of fertile land, developed for farming, were held between its great meandering loops. A final swaying wooden bridge and we were ascending once more but this time to the River View Restaurant; a delicious lunch of thick potato soup, toast and coffee fortified us for the last leg of the uphill climb to the main road, where a driver and car offered the comfort of collapse on the last leg to Kathmandu.

However, things did not go according to plan. At about 35 km from Kathmandu the road was suddenly blocked and traffic in both directions at a standstill. Finally, the driver reported that during the afternoon, while overtaking a car, a bus had accidently knocked down and killed four local people. The angry and desolate villagers had reacted by stopping all the traffic. Mayhem resulted. Then a storm added to the chaos. It took the police another three hours to get the traffic moving. Alternately sleeping and attempting to move and change our positions to release cramp in the legs – the downhill journey had become a staircase to the underworld. Added to this, to survive the nightmare of noise and black fumes from lorries and buses we resorted to holding sweaters over our mouths and noses to avoid choking. When we finally arrived at the guest house it was to find our room occupied. We were taken to a hotel on the outskirts of Kathmandu. It was a welcome relief to discover it was equipped with all mod cons including the luxury of hot water and a bath.

The following morning we had recovered sufficiently to visit the old part of the city. Ancient buildings in various stages of collapse, sporting exquisitely carved surrounds to windows and doorways, looked onto a huge square which served as a market place for stalls overflowing with carved masks and figures; a range of irresistible art pieces competed with bronze sculptures. A confessed addict my interest ranges from the hand carved windows and doors of ancient Omani stone built houses to the massive sombre totems on Easter Island, to the smallest wild animals strung from key rings; on this occasion I succumbed to various combinations of cross-legged meditating Buddhas – bowed heads cupped in the Buddha's hands were cradled between his knees. Back in the vicinity of the guesthouse we explored nearby streets before the luxury of lunch in a garden courtyard serenaded by quiet jazz music.

On our final afternoon we travelled by tuk-tuk along pot-holed roads to the famous Monkey Temple near the city centre. The steps leading to the gold spire were lined with beggars and local people intent on selling gimmicky objects as well as opportunistic monkeys. The reward: spectacular views across Kathmandu Valley – the start of the staircase where glimpses of heaven tug on the heart but remain tantalisingly out of reach.

Return to Tioman Island

Jungle-clad mountains, waterfalls and fast flowing streams; white beaches descend to clear aquamarine bays and turquoise sea where turtles, coral and a wide range tropical fish can be seen by snorkelling just metres off-shore ...

Seletar Airport's informal and jungle-clad surrounds prepared me for my return to Tioman Island. My first visit to this idyllic island, set off the east coast of Malaysia, took place more than a decade ago. On that occasion I was stationed in Singapore. Now, from my base in Dubai, I was on my way to meet up with expatriate friend Isobel, to once again enjoy the beauty of one of the world's most unspoilt and magical places. Built by the British, just before the Second World War, the airport served as a military base until 1968 when it was handed over to the Civil Aviation Authority of Singapore. Used mostly by flying schools and for short distance chartered flights – it was a convenient and atmospheric place for the last leg of my journey.

As the plane descended over the turtle-shaped island, the sight of Dragon Horn Hill's twin peaks disappearing into the flat base of towering cumulus cloud stirred layers of memory. Forested slopes, disentangled from cloud, fell to the coastline where I could make out the stilt houses of a kampong and then the blue rectangle of a pool. Losing height we followed the rugged coastline but I could see nowhere safe to land; minutes later, we were making for a narrow runway lying parallel to the beach, touched down and rumbled to a halt. Isobel was waiting to meet me. Tioman had become her adopted summer holiday home.

Over the past years resorts on the west coast have developed facilities for tour groups for diving and snorkelling as well as a mixture of lively bars for evening entertainment. However, if you want to get away from it all then Juara, on the less accessible east coast and facing the South China Sea, is the place to head for. This was our destination. A forty minute boat-ride later we were approaching the perfect curve of Baruk Beach and tucked behind a fringe of coconut palms, with a backdrop of dark green forest was Bushman Bar, recommended for the excellence of its cuisine. The sun was out, the air clean and bright. Trees were laden with fruit: mango, papaya, banana while flamboyant flowering shrubs grew between chalets on stilts, each with a verandah facing the sea. One of these was to be my home for the next ten days.

Dawn arrived in fiery glory. Apart from the shushing of waves, the occasional throbbing of a boat's engine and the rustling of wind through coconut leaves the only sound was the cry of the Tiong bird. Legend has it that a visitor to the island met a local man, who had a bird perched on his shoulder. The visitor approached the man to ask the name of the island. The man, who thought the visitor was referring to the bird, replied 'Tioman' – meaning my tio bird. Thus the island received its name. Unique to this island, the haunting cry of the bird 'tio, tio' echoes across the sky adding to the sense of magic.

Swimming and snorkelling from the beach or a boat were daily activities. Memories of the paradisiacal underworld of fish and corals, from my previous visit, were still with me. Although Tioman has suffered the effects from increased numbers of divers, rising sea temperatures and a recent monstrous monsoon there were definite signs that the damaged coral is recovering. The fish are still there and care is now taken with special mooring points for diving boats to protect the coral.

However, the island offers the visitor more than the sea to explore. Inland it is home to a variety of wild life including monkeys, flying squirrels, mouse deer, monitor lizards, bats as well as a wide variety of exotic birds and butterflies. One expedition, a jungle-mountain trek to a waterfall on Mentawak River, started with an aerobic bicycle ride through the kampong, which lies a few metres from the beach, at the foot of the mountain. With Isobel taking the lead we set off towards encroaching jungle. The bikes were not new and mine had no brakes turning the ride along jungle tracks and over rattling wooden bridges, with no sides, into something of an assault course.

Breathless, we arrived at the estuary to find that the tide was high. We needed to be on the other side of the river and the only way to cross and keep our cameras and picnic dry was by canoe. There was one problem. We could see the bright red canoe but it was tied to rocks on the opposite bank. I didn't argue when Isobel volunteered to swim across and rescue the canoe. This accomplished, I clambered in and we paddled across ready to begin our trek. Adventures collecting, boarding and leaving the canoe ensured our clothes were wet but in the steamy heat it made a welcome and cool start.

The ascent, in three stages up a track through primary jungle, is edged by a great steep-sided river valley that has been used to install a water pipe from a hydro-electric power station. Trees struggled for light, some soaring hundreds of metres from the valley sides. An eagle was lazily riding thermals overhead while dancing round us varieties of huge brightly coloured butterflies – never still long enough to be photographed – continued to amaze and delight. As we climbed higher and looked back we caught occasional glimpses of the receding South China Sea.

We could hear the rush and tumble of water long before we reached the falls, then we came upon a cluster of empty mineral bottles, upside down on sticks like forgotten fireworks, marking the entrance. It was a dark, damp and eerie place, almost swallowed by surrounding jungle. In spite of the noise the falls were not that high but separated from a series of smaller falls by a tumble of rocks and pools suitable for a refreshing ice-cold dip before our picnic lunch. Strange colourless fish darted in shadowy water. The only place where light seeped through was between curtains of parted leaves over the falling water.

It was one of those days when the sun goes in and out as if controlled by a light switch. I wanted a photograph of light slicing through the trees onto falling water. This entailed a further assault course. Climbing from rock to slippery rock over deep water, I was trying to keep my camera dry and searching for a safe position in readiness for the next explosion of light. Finally, I was perched on a rock mid-falls and before long the sun obligingly lit the stage pausing just long enough for my shot.

While we were enjoying our picnic and listening to birdcalls and rustlings against the rush of water Isobel explained that telephones had been installed in Juara, for the first time, only a few months ago and in that short time, it is said that a bird had learnt to make a perfect imitation of the sound. With memories of David Attenborough's presentation of the lyrebird in the 'Life of Birds' series, I was all ears. The remarkable lyrebird's ability to imitate twenty other bird calls, plus human sounds – such as a camera shutter clicking, a car alarm and a chain saw – gave credence to Isobel's story. With thoughts of the possibility of hearing the sound of a telephone echoing from the tree tops we began our descent.

A further trek, this time to the most well-known waterfall on the Besar River, was memorable for its deep jungle surrounds. We cycled through the kampong of stilt houses but this time in the opposite direction to the start of a narrow path that crosses the mountain to the resort of Tekek. This was the only route to the west side of the mountain and the only way out during the monsoon when the sea is too rough for boats. Great clumps of giant bamboo line the pathway; huge trees, some with girths of up to 6 feet, rise 50-80 metres from the valley floor while giant creepers strangle plants and clothe trees with waterfalls of leaves as if painstakingly arranged for display. Beyond the jungle, the sloping hillside – once covered in plantations of rubber trees – has now been cleared for crops of mangoes.

Once again it was the bird calls that surprised – on this occasion, the strange whooping of the ghost bird. Then rustlings overhead revealed a bushy-coated black squirrel with a tan belly, leaping and hanging from swaying branches. Great swathes of leaves, laced by munching insects, draped around us like impressionist paintings while at our feet beautiful, and almost luminous, green ferns vied for attention.

A boat trip to Coral Island brought back vivid memories of my first Tioman visit. The pure white sands of this beautiful and uninhabited island and its offshore rocky outcrops, spectacular for snorkelling and diving, give it priority status. But it was not memories of the colourful underwater life that had stayed with me as much as an unexpected encounter with a huge monitor lizard. Like many tropical islands, Coral Island has a central crown of rocks and jungle. Drawn towards it to escape the heat and explore I had gone no more than a few paces inside when I came upon a huge primeval creature, forked tongue flicking, as it picked its way heavily over fallen trees and through tangled lianas. Mesmerised, I watched until the end of its dragging tail had disappeared into the undergrowth. My long-lasting regret has been that, at the time, I was without my camera.

I was never without my camera on this trip and determined to capture a monitor lizard on film. Our first hunt, along the estuary of the Baruk River, led to the discovery of footprints leading from the earlier high-tide mark of the river to the edge of the jungle; deeply-bedded at the start, the prints were separated by a wavy line left by the lizard's dragging tail and showed clearly the thumb-like image of the outside toe.

Once again it was a trip to Coral Island that provided a second close encounter. It was late afternoon when the two dive boats of tourists had departed and quiet returned that we decided to explore. Before long we found prints in the sand skirting the jungle. Then we caught sight of a lizard, perfectly still, apart from sensing our presence with its flicking tongue – then another, some two metres long, making its way over the sand. Although smaller than the lizard from my previous encounter, capturing it on film was reward enough.

As an end to a perfect day we made a detour to the resort of Salang where, accustomed to the presence of people, lizards have become scavengers and swim openly in the murky waters of the river. When we had exhausted our lust for shots we relaxed with ice-cold beers from one of the many bars in the busy resort before making our escape.

My final mission was a hunt for pythons. A visitor had reported that while canoeing on the Mentawak River she had sighted a huge coiled python sleeping on a branch overhanging the water. With this in mind we made three canoe trips. We never sighted a python but we did experience the incredible silence of a jungle river broken only by exotic birdsong; the sound of a breeze sifting through leaves and the rasping of the saw-edges of bamboo like falling rain; we heard our paddles stroking the water as we passed a great bush of pale yellow roses. We watched huge butterflies flutter from the riverbanks, opening and closing like bright turquoise and orange flowers or flaunting velvet black bird-wings. We saw ancient forest reflected in dark water and through tangles of lianas, hanging from the tunnel of leaves, great rope-like structures twisting among the foliage – the coiled end of one resembling the head and neck of a resting snake. We kept perfectly still absorbing the quiet – the air filled with the most exquisite perfume – and watched where the undergrowth moved into place when an unseen creature retreated at our passing.

I can imagine no setting as magical for sundowners as the open verandah of Bushman Bar. As shadows grow longer and the sea turns a deeper shade of blue, ice tinkles against glass and the smell of barbequed fish wafts upon the air; soundless as shadows bats appear to weave intricate circles round us, so close that, at times, I have to guard against an instinct to move away. The pattern of their circles grows wider like ripples on water, then tighter. The copper glow of Mars lifts from the horizon in a sky heavy with stars. As darkness thickens, from distant tall trees we hear the wild screeching of fruit bats and watch their huge shadows streak the evening sky as they retreat into the mystical silence of the natural world.

*****

Back in the Emirates, dry heat and a panorama of high-rise blocks edging across the rapidly disappearing ocean of dunes replaced steamy forested slopes cradling pristine beaches; whenever the opportunity arose – to escape the growing nightmare of development – Richard and I packed our two man tent, cool boxes of supplies, bottles of frozen water and our cameras into our beloved Musso (4x4) and headed over one of the borders into unspoilt neighbouring Oman. Among the regions that we had explored Musandam

271

Peninsula was the place we most loved to visit – on this occasion it was for a final farewell.

The Magic of Musandam

On one side a vertical wall of rock towered out of sight, on the other the rock wall fell away to the deep blue of the Arabian Gulf. Gouged into the side of the mountain the road wound round hairpin bends that, at times, followed natural folds in fractured walls of uplifted rock and at others headed along paths bulldozed straight through the mountain. We swung round successive bends, one minute heading perilously towards the ocean and the next into the mountain wall. Overhead, great blocks of undercut stone balanced precariously on ledges. Below smashed boulders littered the roadside – a warning of untimely avalanches. We were approaching Khasab the capital of Musandam, Oman's northern mountain stronghold – just a few hours by road from Dubai.

Ruus Al Jibal – Peaks of the Mountains – was the Arabic name for this isolated mountainous peninsula. Situated at the northern extremity of the Hajar range jutting into the narrow neck of the Arabian Gulf the region is known, today, as Musandam a derivation of *Sanadin* or Anvil's Head after a craggy islet at the peninsula's tip.

In the 16th century the Portuguese made Hormuz into a great trading centre, receiving pearls from Bahrain and the coastal towns, dates from Mesopotamia and incense from inland tribes. Today, this former stronghold of the Persian kings of Hormuz belongs to Oman and offers spectacular mountain scenery and a coastline of magnificent fiords scattered with isolated villages accessible only by sea. Relatively unknown to the world and still in the early stages of organised tourism, Musandam remained wondrously unspoilt.

Our objective was to reach the Tulip Hotel before sunset. Set on a peninsula of rock overlooking the Strait of Hormuz, the hotel's spectacular and isolated setting provided a luxury base for the steadily increasing flow of travellers. We were not newcomers to Musandam, Richard and I had been regular visitors to the Khasab: a comfortable guesthouse with a central courtyard and swimming pool, fringed by a row of palms, silhouetted against a backdrop of mountains. We had enjoyed its informality and lovely setting. Now that it's long and solitary reign had been challenged by a new resort and the advent of tourism, it was under renovation. We couldn't complain. The view from the balcony of our room, at the recently opened hotel, overlooked sea and mountains and sky – it was the perfect place to plan tomorrow's expedition.

The winding track that took us from sea level through Wadi Khasab continued on a steep zig-zagging course finally cresting a ridge that overlooked the wide bowl of the Sayh Plateau. Cradled within the mountains, at 1,800 metres, rust-gold ready for harvest fields, spread before us. Walled terraces of crops, cut into the hillsides, led down to a lake of green criss-crossed by fences dividing fields of wheat, alfalfa, onions and other root crops. A long tradition of trapping rainwater in cisterns for the cultivation of crops, as well as the ancient *falaj* system of channelling water – introduced by the Persians – is still used. From time to time, but especially during the hot dry summer months, farmers from the plateau migrate to the coast to supplement their diet with harvested dates or freshly caught fish, returning to their mountain habitat with supplies of dried fish and dates in time to plant winter crops. Though many villagers have migrated permanently to larger coastal settlements, well-tended fields and some sizeable villas indicated the continuing presence of a successful and established farming community.

Our route into the mountains continued to wind uphill reaching to 1,980 metres at Jebel Harim. It was in this less than hospitable yet magnificent rugged terrain we first noticed neat stone walls marking the entrances to cave dwellings once inhabited by members of the Shihuh. An ancient mountain tribe – said to be descendants of prehistoric immigrants from India, they used caves or simple stone structures as shelters and to store their supplies of food. Feared by other tribal groups as well as by sailors seeking shelter in rocky inlets on the coast, the Shihuh developed a reputation for fierceness.

On his mid-twentieth century travels in Oman, Ronald Codrai met and lived with members of the Shihuh. He believed their reputation was unjustified and that their fearsome behaviour was brought about by their own fear of potential enemies who threatened their frugal existence. It was the threat of attack that led them to remain out of sight exchanging eerie warning calls which reverberated like the cry of wolves through the otherwise silent mountains. When they appeared over ridges, brandishing *jirz*, distinctive traditional axes, it was to protect their families or meagre supplies.

Such was the isolation of the Shihuh that until a decade or so ago, when the convention still existed, if you wanted to approach a Shihuh village, you fired your rifle while some way off as a way of knocking on the door. The people would look out to see who was there before coming to greet their visitors. Nevertheless, their grunts and shrill calls, whether warning or celebratory, did instil fear. One story told is that a group of Shihuh sent to help the Sultan's forces against the imam's insurgents in the late 1950s, so terrified local people with their calls that they were relieved of their duties and sent back to their mountain stronghold.

To this day, the older generation of Omani males walking the streets of Khasab, continue to carry the small axe head or *jirz* – a metre long stick with a blade at the tip. Whether used as a walking aid or a tool for cutting or for protection, it is as much an Omani tradition in Musandam as the decorative curved dagger, the *khanjar*, is to the rest of Oman.

On the far side of Jebel Harim, we followed a narrow ridge that descends to the Rawdah Bowl – a wide open valley scattered with acacia trees and home to people still living in traditional mountain villages but with the undeniable asset of owning a 4WD. Long before the sound of an engine can be heard reverberating through the mountains a whirlwind of dust heralds its approach. We watched a ball of dust bowling across the plain. At its closest crossing point to our own cloud of dust a friendly arm was thrust through the open window to wave. The mountain ridge continued following the course of the deeply gouged Wadi Bih through the Hajar range to the east coast Emirate of Fujairah.

Among the most outstanding views is one that looks down on a range of bare mountains their sides marked by concentric bands of jutting rock, like perfectly executed contour lines.

Even more remarkable are the locations of ancient agricultural sites, situated either at the very bottom of an apparently inaccessible wadi floor or crowning an equally inaccessible hilltop. Oval in shape, to accommodate the rugged surroundings, their levelled sandy floors outlined by neat stone walls remain intact: testimony to an abandoned way of life. Once, ancient tribes shared these mountains with the Arabian leopard. Today, the tribes have migrated and settled in more hospitable terrain and goats outnumber by far the few remaining critically endangered leopard.

We knew that the mountains were inhabited by prehistoric tribes long before the arrival of the Shihuh and were intent on finding evidence of their lives. Just a few kilometres from Khasab on the coast road we followed a track into a wadi leading to the village of Tawi. Opposite a natural well – *tawi* – from which the village has taken its name, stood a tumble of massive boulders. Right before us, on a smooth-faced wall of rock, was the legacy of rock art left by ancient people. Camels, boats and warriors or huntsmen on horseback were clearly marked and easily accessible from ground level.

Within minutes we were surrounded by curious villagers. The younger girls spoke some English, and pointed to the position of artwork on higher boulders not easily seen from the ground. I followed in Richard's wake as he climbed to a viewing point between precariously balanced boulders. Pecked with flint-stone on rock walls, the engravings confirmed prehistoric man's use of boats and horses for trade and travel. Equally remarkable and thought provoking was the similarity between these engravings and those we had seen on rocks in Wadi Daykah, some two hours drive south of Muscat. Scenes of people hunting and warriors riding on camels and horses appeared identical to the petroglyphs before us now: confirmation that the same people travelled long distances through desert and mountains and from Tawi continued their travels and trading by and from the sea.

On our return we stopped to admire the shadow of Khasab Fort. Overlooking an inlet and against a backdrop of barren mountains, it stands guard over the old settlement as it has done for centuries past. The irregular shape and appearance of four corner towers and adjoining walls, built by the Portuguese in the seventeenth century is supplemented by the massive central tower in the main courtyard. Like that of Nizwa Fort, the tower is believed to be of Persian origin and to predate the castle itself. Ceilings, filled in with plaited palm fronds and mud, supported by teak timbers brought from India, are just one more reminder of the trade and interchange of goods made easier by the fort's optimum coastal position. Once an essential supply point for dates and water for Portuguese trading ships, it has remained in constant use, serving as residence for the *Wali* – the local governor – and as a jail for prisoners, before becoming the museum that it is today.

Mist and clouds from the mountains greeted us on the following morning. Nevertheless, we were determined to take a dhow ride into one of the many isolated inlets on the coast. En route we passed a bay next to the port, quite literally filled with small speed boats: a reminder that Khasab was and is an Iranian smuggling den. Sheep and goats are brought into this bay and exchanged for American cigarettes and electronic goods. On the return trip, assets wrapped in black plastic, the smugglers head back after dark, some 55 km across the strait in high powered boats. Iranian coastguards as well as other shipping have to be avoided. With so many tankers passing to and fro the crossing is hazardous. Both Omanis and Iranians are said to be quite open about and to benefit from this 'illegal' trade.

Finally, we located our dhow and, given the poor weather conditions, decided on a half-day trip into the nearby sound of Khor ash Sham. Ali, our skipper-cum-owner, a native of Kumzar, the remote village set in an isolated cove on the most northern tip of the peninsula, was familiar with every secret inlet in the fiords. A gentle and courteous man he smiled and shrugged his shoulders when we asked if there was truth in the rumour that the people of his village were descendants of shipwrecked sailors. Traditionally a fishing village and isolated from outside human contact for thousands of years, the inhabitants still speak a language of their own.

'Today,' Ali said, 'my people speak Arabic and our language – some Persian, English, Portuguese, French... They have school, small hospital and electricity. To my village by boat, two hour.'

Furnished with Persian rugs and floor cushions, Ali's dhow was his prized possession. He treated us like honoured guests, offering miniature glasses of hot sweet tea, water and fresh fruit. On a day trip barbequed fish is served with salad and Arabic bread for lunch. In common with most converted dhows, an engine replaced sails and an upright 'coffin' in the stern housed primitive but adequate toilet facilities.

Rolling mist and cloud clothed the mountains and fiords. Temperatures apart, it could have been Scotland or Norway itself. On sunny days the crystal waters are so clear that coral and tropical fish can be seen from the deck. Then it is not unusual to be accompanied by turtles, reef sharks or dolphins while many other exotic varieties of tropical sea-life can be seen while snorkelling. However, there was something mysterious and appropriate about the mist-clad *khors* (fiords) creating an atmosphere well suited to tales of smugglers and pirates who used to hide in the secret inlets.

Isolated villages fringing the sound have taken strides into the modern world. Concrete square houses with satellite TV receivers replaced the ruins of former stone-built homes that blended into the rugged background. Pylons, miraculously striding over mountain peaks, carry electric power to the village.

'Children have school in Khasab – by boat,' Ali explained, 'and water for village come by boat,' he added pointing to a huge blue tank strategically stationed on the stony beach.

Our tour took us past a barren and isolated rocky outcrop. Situated in the inlet of Khor ash Sham, on a bend at the tip of a remote peninsula invisible from the sea, it was the notorious Telegraph Island. A flight of worn stone steps led to the remains of stone walls that marked the former British Telegraph Station. It was from this remote outpost that engineers passed the first telegraphic message from London to Karachi in 1865. The achievement took its toll on the engineers. Assigned to this barren outcrop for tours of duty lasting for six months, the men suffered from a form of isolation madness that became known as 'going round the bend' – a saying that is used to this day to describe the onset of varieties of madness.

As we left the inhospitable island, sunlight filtering through cloud gave shape to the mountains and depth to the water. A touch of magic was added when the resident school of dolphins broke the surface to greet us and then escorted us back to the port.

One minute we were climbing a steep sandy track and the next we crested a ridge and drew to a sudden halt. Below us, stretched between the arms of a ring of mountains, lay the aquamarine waters of a magnificent fiord. It was the sand spits and *khors* of Musandam Peninsula and the adjacent coast that enabled pirates from the seventeenth to the nineteenth centuries to escape capture. Hiding in concealed inlets they fell upon their prey, escaping again when chased by warships.

Today, great fingers of green merged with blue reaching between amber slopes to distant hidden coves that sheltered isolated villages, before opening to the jaws of the Indian Ocean. This was Khor Najd – the only fiord accessible from inland and a photographer's dream. I knew that attempts to capture the sheer size and wonder of it were bound to fail. So it remains, imperfectly reproduced on film, a perfect living memory of the magic of Musandam.

Dipping into Dorset

Yachts, with sails full blown, race against a backdrop of sand-fringed bays, coves and islands: a seascape that viewed from the air could be mistaken for the Bahamas. In fact, it is not the Caribbean but a bird's eye view of the coastline of Dòrset, England's loveliest county.

As the bronze sun melts into the horizon and the last of the yachts stream past the waiting ferry and through the inlet into Poole Harbour – the second biggest natural harbour in the world – we make our way along millionaire row. This is Sandbanks where a beach-hut without running water or electricity costs hundreds of thousands of English pounds and where a waterfront house is currently up for sale for 11.5 million. I first visited Dorset and bought a home there after staying with friends from wind-surfing days in Singapore. It was the place I fell in love with and that Richard and I returned to when 'on leave': a lovely and convenient base to recover and meet up with family and friends, as well as to plan further travels.

It didn't take long to discover that Dorset has everything going for it including the most hours of sunshine in the UK and so many designated areas of outstanding natural beauty that it's difficult to know which direction to take. Its chequered and fascinating history including the coming and going of invaders, settlers and explorers is just as intriguing. Just a few miles inland on the northern edge of Purbeck, we set our sights on the Anglo-Saxon walled town of

Wareham. Surrounded by marshes and with streets laid out like a chessboard, the town, which marks the highest bridging point on the River Frome, was once Dorset's port.

At Wareham Quay, with its cobbled square overlooking the river, we locate and head for the upmarket Priory Hotel. Like the town the hotel is steeped in history; dating from the early 16th century, for five hundred years there were monks in residence and before that a convent of nuns. A Carthusian Priory stood on the site until the dissolution of the monasteries in 1539 when parts of the priory lodgings were turned into an inn. The present tastefully converted building overlooks four acres of beautiful gardens – all that remains of former extensive monastic lands. With an afternoon to dispose of we indulge in a glass of wine and lunch on a flower-decked terrace, overlooking open countryside and the river before exploring.

Wareham once boasted seven churches. Of the three surviving St Martins – dating from 1030 – it is believed to be built on the site of a Roman Temple and to be the only Saxon church in Dorset which remains in anything like its original form. In addition to 12th century wall frescoes – one depicting Saint Martin on horseback, dividing his cloak to give one half to a naked beggar – the added bonus is that the church houses an effigy of a man dressed in Arab robes.

Armed with a large metal key, on loan from the vicar, we locate the church at the narrowest point of the high street and enter; with the aid of a leaflet guide we follow directions to the north wall of the 11th Century Chancel to gaze upon and interpret the fresco of Saint Martin before making our way to stand before the life-size sculpture. The remarkable effigy before us, portraying a man lying on a stone sarcophagus, his head on a camel's saddle, his hand on an Arab dagger in the pose of a medieval crusader is none other than that of Lawrence of Arabia. It was along the road leading to the nearby Bovington military training ground that 46 year old Thomas Edward Lawrence lost his life in 1935. A monument marks the spot where, thrown off his motorbike, he crashed into a tree while swerving to miss two cyclists.

Lawrence met his untimely death on his way to Clouds Hill – the cottage where he hoped to find peace after years of guerrilla warfare and to establish himself as a writer. The following day we join a steady stream of people who had come to visit his humble home, set at the foot of the hill it was named after. Well-stocked bookshelves, a gramophone and a comfortable fireside leather couchette, occupying the larger part of the downstairs lounge, appeared to offer a place to rest and compose. It was here that he finished writing his remarkable account of the Arab Revolt, *The Seven Pillars of Wisdom*.

Our pilgrimage continued to the churchyard in Moreton where on an open stone book, lying at the foot of Lawrence's narrow grave, the words DOM MINA INVS TIO ILLV MEA – The Lord is my light – have been engraved: the motto of Oxford University where, as a student of archaeology, Lawrence wrote a thesis on the influence of the Crusades on medieval military architecture in Europe. In late afternoon sunlight it was a sobering and atmospheric place.

Next on our itinerary was a visit to the house and gardens of the magnificent stately mansion of Kingston Lacy. The house and its history cannot fail to impress while, within its walls is a treasure trove of souvenirs collected by the late owner, historian and traveller William Bankes. Built by Sir Ralph Bankes in 1663, after his parents' former home – none other than historic Corfe Castle – was destroyed by the Roundheads, under the orders of parliament during the English Civil War. Kingston Lacy and the remains of Corfe Castle remained in the ownership of the Bankes family until 1982 when both were bequeathed as part of the Kingston Lacy and Corfe Castle Estate to the National Trust.

This was not my first visit to Kingston Lacy – on this occasion my interest and focus were not on the house and the magnificent display of souvenirs collected on William Bankes' travels but on an even grander souvenir – an ancient Egyptian obelisk. While Richard – binoculars trained on a hovering buzzard – strolled towards the ha-ha fringing the gardens I made my way down a gravel path leading from the very centre of the house to the impossible to miss monument.

From the seventeenth to the nineteenth centuries it became both lucrative and fashionable to ship artefacts from Egypt and the Graeco-Roman sites to Europe. Literally hundreds of columns, left lying about the vandalised ancient sites, were collected and transported notably to France and England where they were used to enhance the palaces of Louise XIV at Versailles and Paris and to create an elegant ruin for George IV at Windsor Castle. The British Museum houses a variety of treasures taken for safe-keeping while others ended up in private houses and gardens including Kingston Lacy.

I have a similar penchant for collecting *objets trouves* on my travels, though of more modest proportions and value. My treasures include a bronze head-hunter's gong, sporting two dragons, purchased from a market stall in Brunei; a whale's vertebrae picked up on a beach in Oman; a remarkable *khanjar* (curved dagger) complete with a rhino horn handle and Jewish-Yemeni writing engraved on the blade, discovered among tourist kitsch, at Sharjah's Blue Souk; my most prized acquisitions: two silver Roman coins – one with an image of the head of the Emperor Septimius Severus (AD 193-211) and one of his wife Julia Domna acquired from a local while exploring Leptis Magna in Libya. These coins and memories of my visit to Leptis Magna explain my interest in the obelisk. I was keen to read the detail engraved on the pedestal explaining the monument's connection with Libya.

From my research I understood that the pink granite 'needle' – dedicated to 'Ptolemy and two Cleopatras, his Queens' was erected by Isis priests on the island of Philae in Egypt, to celebrate exemption from paying tax. Discovered and laid claim to by William Bankes in 1815 – it then took seven years to transport the obelisk from Egypt to Kingston Lacy; during this time it was subjected to a number of traumas including falling into the Nile while being loaded onto a boat and being the object of a gun battle with rival Egyptologists. Such was the damage suffered that serious repair work was necessary before it could be raised to stand unaided.

Finally, I located the explanation I was seeking, engraved on the pedestal at the foot of the monument:

'the granite used in the reparation of the monument was brought from the remains of Leptis Magna in Africa and was given for that purpose by his majesty King George IV'

Just standing before the obelisk took me back to my travels to the ancient Egyptian then Graeco-Roman cities stringing Libya's coastline; in particular the memory of the life-size bronze statue of the Emperor Septimius Severus standing, one hand in a gesture of giving, before the Triumphal Arch, at the entrance to the once magnificent city of Leptis Magna; Leptis – the place of the emperor's birth – was the city he loved and had returned to embellish. Thanks to the Italians – during their war-time occupation of Libya – those areas of the city that had not been pillaged have undergone splendid restoration. In this instance, it was as a result of the removal and transportation of ruins from Leptis that the obelisk before me had been restored.

I circled the monument. It was not difficult to locate the eroded cup shaped joining seam in the lower section of the needle where it clipped the tail end of the hieroglyphs, plus a lower seam where the

Leptis granite was attached to the pedestal; the seams, plus the lighter colour of the added stone, made it clear that extensive repairs had been carried out: confirmation that without this restoration work the obelisk would not be standing. Mission accomplished, camera in hand I set off to join Richard. My plan, to find the best location for capturing an image of the obelisk with the stately mansion in the background, was thwarted by an unexpected downpour of rain.

*****

From ancient Egyptian artefacts to Shaftesbury – the only hilltop town in Dorset with spectacular views over Blackmore Vale. Along with Sherborne, Shaftsbury was one of the focal points of the rise of England's medieval monasteries as well as of their dramatic destruction by Parliamentary forces during the Civil War. Once a centre of monastic life and a popular place of pilgrimage, Shaftsbury is now home to the remains of a Benedictine Abbey.

From Abbey Walk, held in place by a buttressed wall and running alongside the former abbey, we look down on a steep cobbled hill. Known as Gold Hill – a corruption of Guild Hall Hill – it is no longer a walk to the abbey but has become a well-known beauty spot for tourists as well as being a favourite location for advertising companies. Seated before the window of a coffee shop, conveniently located at the very top of the hill, with perfect views of the row of terraced houses that stagger down one side and the towering brick wall demarcating the other, I could understand why.

We head south, allowing for a stop at the village of Bere Regis. My focus was the village church of St John the Baptist and my addiction for wood carvings. Traced back to Saxon then Norman times, today the main glory of this church is the magnificent carved and painted roof given by a Cardinal Morton in 1485. Among the notable carvings within the church, the full length figures of the twelve apostles – carved in oak and looking down from dragon beams on either side of open roof trusses – were my priority; among them I indentified Peter by his mitre and the keys he is carrying and Judas Iscariot by his money bag. I was not disappointed.

As its given name, The Ghost Village, suggests Tyneham is no ordinary village. Intrigued by stories of this lost or ghost settlement we set off to explore. Nestling in a valley below the steep slopes of Whiteway Hill we came upon former houses and shops that time and weather have reduced to collapsed roofs between crumbling walls. In contrast the nearby church and schoolhouse – though unused and unlived in – have been preserved as they were left years ago. Poignant images of pupils' names over their coat pegs as well as work in progress left on their desks in the simple schoolhouse building stay with me. The story told is that in 1939, at the start of Second World War, the Ministry of Defence decided to take over the village for the duration of the war and promised the villagers that they could have their homes back when the war ended. This never happened, the area is still held and used by the MOD and the lost village remains deserted to this day.

Leaving the village we followed the skyline to the edge of Whiteway Hill where it drops precipitously to the sea hundreds of feet below. A foot path follows the cliff edge – just one of Dorset's many lovely coastal walks – down to a sand-fringed bay. The next headland along will take us back to the near start of our trip. Beyond the promontory of rocks lies Lulworth Cove and then on to Poole Harbour for a planned *rendezvous* at the Haven Hotel

*****

A lasting memory of my visit to Tyneham is especially pertinent for a photograph I took of the church. Later, that day, when I was looking over the selection of shots I was astonished to see an image – taken of my six year old granddaughter on a swing in my garden, on the previous day – was super-imposed on the photograph of the church. It was as if an apparition of a child from the past had appeared within the walls of the church. This double image in my camera has never happened before or since.

Afterword

November 2014: on a return visit to Kingston Lacy in order to photograph the obelisk, I arrived to find it completely surrounded by scaffolding. Once again my photographic mission was thwarted. From my investigations, I learnt that a team – from Oxford University – were using new imaging techniques to reveal Greek markings on the base that were previously too worn to investigate. With the aid of these techniques the team was intent on comparing the translated Greek inscriptions with those of the Egyptian hieroglyphs. In fact, it was the hieroglyphs and Greek inscriptions on the obelisk that helped 19th century scholars unlock the secrets of trilingual writings of the Rosetta Stone[8], revealing an understanding of lost civilisations. This inspired the European Space Agency to name the 21st century space mission, to unlock the secrets of the universe – Rosetta Mission; while its space lander craft, destined to land on a comet far from Earth, has been named Philae – in honour of the obelisk.

Such is the excitement over this project that space agency scientists and Egyptologists met on the lawn of this country estate to highlight the link between the planned trip to the stars and the celebrated 19th century adventurer, William Bankes.

> November 12th 2014. The successful if troubled landing of the Philae lander resulted in the probe beaming back a wealth of information during its short initial life on the comet. This, in turn, will enable scientists to unlock some of the secrets of the origins of the universe, confirming the mission's link with Kingston Lacy's Philae obelisk.

---

[8] Ancient stele with Egyptian trilingual text, housed in the British Museum since 1802

Summer Snow in Andalusia

One of the most famous white villages of the Axarquia, Competa
glistens against the impressive backdrop of the Sierras.

The road climbed and twisted round hairpin bends for over 600 metres until we were looking down on Competa. New development snaked from the old, reaching up and round, spreading across the hillside like gigantic tentacles; another bend then the road dropped and became a track leading to our mountain retreat, perched like an eerie on the side of the Sierra Almijara. Less than an hour's drive from Malaga yet the setting was remote and came with views across the Sierras to the Mediterranean Sea. Immersed in an unimaginable quiet broken only by the shrill of cicadas we watched swallows streaking the sky – dipping and swooping against a canopy of deepening blue.

The start of our trip did not go according to our plans. The hire care that we had reserved to pick up at Malaga Airport was not there. In the end we took a taxi to the hotel. On the following day we hired another taxi back to the airport; this time the car was ready and waiting. Mishap number two: when we finally located the house in Gaucin – belonging to expatriate friends from Dubai we had planned to visit – there was no-one in. Somehow we must have got the dates wrong and ended up putting a note, with our contact details, through the letter box of their empty abode.

We spent a couple of days recovering and absorbing the peace of our surroundings as well as enjoying the cool waters of the gravity-defying swimming pool tucked into the hillside; it also gave us time to plan excursions to some of the ancient and fortified hilltop towns and villages strung along the dramatic landscape of the Southern Sierras. First on the agenda was the market town of Antequera. Strategically important, first as the Roman town of Anticaria and later as the Moorish border fortress Antequera defending the approach to Granada before the conquest by Christian rulers – the sense of history in reverse to that of Istanbul was before us.

Narrow streets radiated from the centre of Antequera, leading to the 13th Century Moorish Castle at one end and to the Plaza de Toros – a museum of bullfighting, at the other. By mid-morning we were enjoying coffee at a roadside café before making our way towards the castle and detouring to photograph a Castilian fortress complete with ornate doorways and arches of ancestral palaces and homes. Artwork and architecture from Roman, Moorish, Renaissance and Baroque periods leapt upon us from all directions. The final approach up a flight of stone steps led to the 16th century Triumphal Arch. However, the most stunning views of the castle, crowning the hill and defending the surrounding white settlement, were undoubtedly those from the road as we neared Torcal Park.

Imposing limestone scenery en route gave us a foretaste of the surreal landscape awaiting us. Great pillars of white rock at once resembled gigantic figures caught in time and a weird lunar landscape. In some places layers of rock balanced precariously one upon the other varying dramatically in size and width so that larger blocks balanced on smaller ones appeared about to topple and shatter. We followed the Green or easy route into the depths of a gorge between intimidating pillars. Then we were climbing uphill again stopping, from time to time, to examine daunting rock sculptures that rose before us and thankful for the cool breeze that fanned the heat. Impressive stacks of tilted rock dominated the brow of the hill. In the distance, across a vista of low-lying hills, a network of lakes has created a wetland that teems with bird life in the spring.

We doubled back, north of Antequera, to find the *Laguna de Fuente* – the pink lagoon – the largest of the lakes. Now, in summer's drought it was reduced to a narrow stretch of water sufficient to satisfy the 100 or so remaining pink flamingoes – that have given the lake its name – and our enthusiasm: long angular legs and strange corkscrew necks were reflected in the mirrored surface.

Low cloud and mist cleared as we approached a huge U-shaped pass through the Sierras leading us to the place where Alhambra balanced precariously on the edge of a gorge. An enclave beneath leafy trees at a loop in the gorge made a perfect picnic spot. To one side the undercut cliff fell into darkness – the other opened to a wide sunlit valley. On the move again we passed a farmhouse with glowing white walls standing guard over a neat grove of olive trees then the road twisted and turned through tiny villages that ended almost as soon as they began. Finally, a dappled avenue of trees formed a perfect tunnel over the road providing a magical end to our detour.

The route to Garganta del Chorro, an immense gaping chasm rising high above the Guadalhorce River, was through a now familiar landscape of limestone peaks and cliffs. A railway line ran along the opposite side of the river crossing arched bridges that stride over deep cuttings then, where the gorge slashes through the mountain, it disappeared into a tunnel. A precipitous catwalk crossed the narrowest point at 180 metres above the churning water. The road took us through pine-clad slopes before descending to lakes of cobalt blue.

On the following day, fortified by a lunch of traditional iced-soup – *Gazpacho* – and tuna salad at a local tapas bar we set off to explore one of the most spectacularly located cities in Andalusia. Set on a massive rocky outcrop Ronda straddles a precipitous limestone cleft and like Competa has all the hallmarks of a classic Moorish *pueblo blanco* (white village): cobbled alleys, window grilles and dazzling whitewash abound. Miraculously, it has evaded becoming a popular tourist venue making it possible to wander through quiet narrow streets enjoying its rich inheritance of art and architecture or to explore the Roman ruins of its more distant past. Inevitably we were drawn to the clusters of buildings straddling Tajo Gorge where the vertical walls of the cliff-edge fall 100 metres to the floor below. Almost impregnable Ronda was one of the last Moorish bastions to fall to the Christians.

Undoubtedly, the remarkable Moorish city of Granada and its fairytale citadel of Alhambra – originally built for the last Muslim emirs in Spain and the court of the Nasrid dynasty – are top of every tour group's agenda. The decision not to visit during summer's tourist madness but to wait for autumn's calm was deliberate. However, we reasoned that crowds in the Sierra Nevada in mid-August were unlikely and maybe I could satisfy a child-like ambition to stand on a remaining pocket of late summer snow.

From Europe's highest road we watched the landscape adopt an open grandeur. Below, whitewashed villages cling to rugged terrain then we rounded a pronounced bend and stopped to admire the green waters of a lake – so still it could have been a painting. Pine forests clothed the sides as we climbed to 1,000, 2,000 and finally 2,500 metres. Before us towered the majestic peaks of Pico Veleta and Mulhacen – between them, on the lower slopes, swathes of snow-filled hollows. We pause on a clump of rocks amidst alpine flowers and butterflies and then set our sights on a distant heart-shaped spread of snow.

Tiny ant-like figures moved across the surface. A cool breeze disguised the strength of the sun as we climbed and slowly the outlines of skiers emerged on the widening white stretch. Nevertheless, it remained disconcertingly distant. Looking down we caught sight of a nearby tongue of snow trapped at the side of a valley. A change of direction and minutes later my wish was granted. Richard was waiting, camera in hand to capture an image of me on a carpet of snow in the Sierra Nevada in mid-August.

Galway in March. Don't Forget Your Umbrella!

Oysters, the Gaelic language, Aran sweaters and rain are as intrinsic to Ireland's west coast as is the wild beauty that stretches between peninsulas of rock left behind when glaciers and ice-sheets stripped the land bare of soil. A landscape of mountains, lakes, rivers and rolling green hills dotted with white-washed farmhouses and littered with dry stone walls divide the land into a patchwork of fields. Vast empty blankets of bog surround the waterways, providing peat to fuel open hearths. We soon discovered that one of the greatest pleasures after returning from a day of mist and cloud and rain sweeping in from the Atlantic, is to sit with glass in hand by the glowing embers of a peat fire.

It was on a day of relentless rain that Richard and I stood on the edge of the Moher Cliffs looking at the sheer drop of over 200 metres to rolling waves exploding in white spray. It is here that the bare face of the great limestone and shale plateau of the Burren meets the full force of the Atlantic. We watched fleeting images of sea birds that colonise the flagstone ledges of the cliff-face before plodding uphill to the highest point. Here, from O'Brien's Tower, we could make out the humped backs of the three Aran Islands, the most remote outposts of Ireland, rising through sea mist like great whales from the ocean.

Bleak and virtually treeless the islands have a fascinating cultural heritage dating back to prehistoric settlements; said to be even more atmospheric are the 6th to 9th century Christian churches established on the islands. The monks located their sanctuaries at pre-Christian ceremonial sites intertwining pagan and early Christian traditions and exerting a magnetic pull to these islands that continues to lure pilgrims, tourists and spiritual healers. Visitors come to meditate and conduct rituals at Celtic Christian centres and even to marry. Recently, a Japanese couple seeking a Celtic wedding took their vows at the monastic ruins on the Aran Island of Inishmore.

The following morning we set off in unexpected sunlight to explore the coastline of Connemara where hundreds of lakes and tiny islands surrounded by bog-land are set against the brooding range of the Twelve Bens and the Maumturk Mountains. Glimpses of superb beaches: huge sweeps of white sand washed by the opalescent waters of the bay – appeared as unreal as they are unspoilt. By the time we had reached the western most village of Clifden clouds were rolling from sea to land, clothing the mountain-tops and blotting out the landscape with sheets of rain.

Just south of Clifden Harbour a signpost caught Richard's eye. 'Alcock & Brown' he enthused screeching to a halt before following the direction of another sign pointing uphill.

'First to fly across the Atlantic' he enlightened me. Minutes later we were confronted by a sculpture of an aeroplane wing – a memorial set up to remember the British adventurers. Further research revealed that in 1919 their daring flight from Newfoundland across the Atlantic ended when in celebration, the intrepid aviators circled Clifden twice then nose-dived into a bog wrecking the plane and their plans to continue their flight to London. The sideways-on monument of a full-size aeroplane wing, carved from limestone and rising from the side of hill overlooking the bog-land, serves as a fitting memorial to the melodramatic arrival of the two heroic survivors.

On our final day we head west once more – this time via Tralee to the Dingle Peninsula celebrated for its panoramic scenery of yet more lakes and mountains as well as a coastline of empty sandy bays and shorelines visited by dolphins and seals. The sun shone as we approached the celebrated Blennerville Windmill; built in 1780 it was restored to full working order in 1984. Today, it marks the gateway to an area renowned for numerous pre-historic and Christian remains, a wealth of Gaelic literature from the Blasket Islands and the fact that 'Ryan's Daughter' and scenes from 'Far and Away' starring Tom Cruise were filmed here.

Our mission: to find further relics of ancient Gaelic culture: ring forts, oratories – small oval shaped churches – and stone crosses, we head for the coast road to Brandon Point. An unexpected encounter with an upside-down figure, legs clad in green Wellington boots and sticking out of a barrel outside Ned Natterjack's Pub at Castlegregory, was the first photo stop. In Ireland quirky humour and culture come side by side with the past. Then minutes later we happened upon ancient relics in a churchyard at Killiney.

Dating from pre-historic times and adopted by modern Christians the older sections of the present day churchyard include the remains of a medieval church and tower as well as stone rectangular family tombs each with a sealed doorway at one end, marked with a ringed iron handle. Among these were several ancient stone-built graves in the shape of a wedge, with one end of the grave higher and wider than its foot. A resident rabbit, disturbed by my presence, dodged out from between the stones of one. Other finds included a moss covered Gaelic cross, an ancient stone cross and a memorial to a family vault – AD 1834 – set into the wall of an ancient ivy-clad building.

Finally we arrive at the headland at Brandon Point overlooking the sweeping bay from where it is believed that St Brendan, the navigator set sail on his voyage of discovery into the western ocean. Legend has it that he discovered the North American continent in the 6th century. The remarkable adventurer and explorer Tim Severin, gave credence to the story by setting sail from Brandon creek in 1977, in a similar vessel to that used by Saint Brendan. Described as the greatest epic voyage in modern Irish history, Tim Severin and his companions built a boat using the same materials – ox hides stitched together in a patchwork and stretched over a wooden frame – and techniques available in the sixth-century AD, then sailed her from Brandon Creek in Dingle to Newfoundland, surviving storms and even a puncture from pack ice.

Disappointed to find that the road to Connor Pass, the highest mountain pass in Ireland was closed we retraced our route through Castle Gregory and made for Dingle and Slea Headland, an area crowded with ancient sites. Once again rolling cloud hid the mountain peaks and brought accompanying sheets of rain. From the mountain road we looked down on the ruins of the remarkable prehistoric stone promontory fort of Dunbeg – a fortified stone wall guarding the remains of a circular building within the enclosure.

Just metres along the road we decide to brave the rain and climbed the hill to a pair of beehive shaped huts. The circular walls, built of overlapping stones, curve gradually inwards to be covered by a corbelled roof – an ingenious technique that goes back to the burial chamber in the great stone tomb at Newgrange, built 5,000 years ago. The style was also reminiscent of the impressive 3rd Millennium BC Beehive Tombs that we had visited in Al Ayn, Oman; the same building technique has been used as for these huts which served as dwellings for local people as well as for monks seeking solitude.

I followed a passageway through the outer circular stone wall into one of the huts. Inside there was plenty of headroom and the inner diameter, of some twelve feet, allowed for a family to shelter and sleep. A further passage lead to an adjoining enclosure thought to have been used for animals. Just as we were completing our photographic activity a voice hailing us through the rain drew our attention to a farmer on his tractor. It was a heritage site and we were expected to give a donation. Wending our way past sheep with thick long-haired coats – living memorials to ancient life in these hills – we make our way to his farmhouse to make our payment.

Our journey continued to the tip of Dunmore Head. Directly below a cauldron of waves exploded against splintered rocks in Blasket Sound where the Armada ships Santa Maria de la Rosa and San Juan were shattered to pieces in 1588. Through driving rain we could make out the great red humps of sandstone rock of the Blasket Islands, once a Viking stronghold.

Back inland, east of Dingle at the village of Annascaul we locate the South Pole Inn. Situated alongside a quietly flowing river – nowhere on earth seemed further from the South Pole. This was the former home of Tom Crean, a local man who rose from the obscurity of a poor farming community in Kerry to become one of the greatest characters in the history of Polar exploration at the turn of the 20th century. Inside, the pub had been transformed into an informal museum with a display of photographs and memorabilia from his Antarctic expeditions. Alongside photographs of Scott and Shackleton, figures everyone recognizes, are images of the 'Unsung Hero' of Michael Smith's book: Tom Crean.

To have ended this trip seated round a peat fire in Galway stirred layers of memory – in particular of my father's Gaelic heritage. As a young man he ran away from his home in Ireland to join the British army. Stationed in Kent he met and married my mother, adding Norman blood to our lineage. Their footsteps and shadows crossed the world to army bases in Egypt, India and then Burma where my life began. We raised our glasses to the memory of the local hero, Tom Crean and to the ghosts and voices that haunt and bring to life the intriguing ancient, lost and changing worlds of our travels.

Selective Bibliography

John Gottenberg Anderson, *Insight Guides, Sri Lanka* (APA Productions, Hong Kong, 1983)

Samuel Israel & Bikram Grewal, *Insight Guides, India* (APA Productions, Hong Kong, 1985)

Hans Johannes Hoefer, *Insight Guides, Malaysia* (APA Productions, Hong Kong, 1987)

Hans Johannes Hoefer, *Insight Guides, Thailand* (APA Productions, Hong Kong, 1988)

Frena Bloomfield, *Post Guide, Thailand* (CFW Publications Ltd, Hong Kong, 1988)

D.E.L. Haynes, *The Antiquities of Tripolitania* (Department of Antiquities, Libya 1981)

James Azema, *Libya Handbook* (Footprint Handbooks Ltd, 2000)

Barth Heinrich, *Travels in North and Central Africa* (Ward, Lock & Co, 1980)

Heiner Klein & Rebecca Brickson, *Off-Road in Oman* (Motivate Publishing, Dubai 1982)

Peter Sager, *The West Country* (Pallas Guides, 1996)

David Baird, *Seville & Andalusia* (Dorling Kindersley Travel Guides, London, 2000)

Margaret Greenwood & Hildi Hawkins, *Ireland* (The Rough Guides, 1994)